"You showed me how to be a better version of myself and for that I am truly grateful."

S.M. - Finance Director

EMPOWERED!

How to change your life in your coffee break

Anne Mulliner

Empowered!

First published in 2014 by

Panoma Press
48 St Vincent Drive, St Albans, Herts, AL1 5SJ, UK
info@panomapress.com
www.panomapress.com

Book layout by Neil Coe

Printed on acid-free paper from managed forests.

Printed and bound in Great Britain by
Marston Book Services Ltd, Oxfordshire

ISBN 978-1-909623-32-3

DEDICATION

This book is dedicated with much love to my lovely mum, Margaret, and my two gorgeous daughters, Charlotte and Elizabeth. Without your love and support none of this would be possible.

ACKNOWLEDGMENTS

I have always had the dream of being a published author and while the birth of this book has not been plain sailing, the experiences that my clients and I share with you in these pages have finally been put out into the real world for consumption.

It would be difficult to write here a fitting acknowledgment to everyone I should include as these acknowledgments could fill a book on their own, but to everyone not specifically mentioned who I have met or worked with in the past please know that you have somewhere, somehow, had an impact on my life and that contribution is reflected somewhere in this book.

I do want to pay special thanks to my parents, Margaret and Brian, and to my brother, Paul, for their continuous love and support. I would also like to make a special mention of gratitude to my amazing network of friends, especially Alison, Amanda, Catherine, Christine, Elizabeth, Helen, Julie, Kate, Lorna, Marmite, Sarah, Susie, Suzanne and Tina – I thank you for your support, love, encouragement and belief at all the different stages of my life when I've been stuck and disempowered and needed reminding there was another way. Thanks goes also to my amazing clients, who continually show what is possible by rising to the challenges they experience and who absolutely live the best lives they can. Special thanks must go to those clients who agreed to their stories being included in this book so that you may benefit from their experiences.

I acknowledge all the team at Panoma Press, and especially Mindy, Bianca and Emma; Without them this book would never have been written. To my team of reviewers – Elizabeth, Helen, Kate and Kelly – I must say thank you for your honesty and care in working on the different sections of the book with me. I am eternally grateful.

And finally to my two beautiful daughters, Charlotte and Elizabeth, you are my inspiration and you undoubtedly help make me the best possible version of myself. I want to thank you for believing in me and for supporting me through the many months of writing. Thank you for making me laugh when I was getting frustrated, for preparing me food when I was getting hungry and for reminding me that, no matter what, the most important job I do is being your mum.

CONTENTS

INTRODUCTION

Do you feel like your life is in a rut? Do you feel like everyone around you is experiencing a better and more fulfilled existence?

Do you people-watch – perhaps in a coffee shop or in a pub or on the tube or when you are on a long drive in the car – and feel a bit envious of what you see in others? Do you consider yourself to be living life at 10 out of 10? If the answer is no – then you have come to the right place.

Over more than 20 years I've met friends, family and clients in coffee shops, offices and restaurants for chats and discussions over a cappuccino or a skinny latte on the meaning of life, why they feel themselves to be stuck in a rut or why they feel that there is something important missing in their lives and what they can do to get moving in a better direction.

I decided to write this book as a resource for if you are questioning who, where or what you are right now. However, this book comes with an extreme warning, as I don't want you to waste your time, effort and money buying it unless you are really clear as to what is on offer here.

This book is *not* for people who:

- are willing to settle

- believe that they are perfect

- believe themselves to have never experienced pain, disappointment and loss

- expect everything to be done for them.

This book *is* for people who:

- want hope, happiness and success

- want answers

- want to follow tried-and-tested strategies in order to get massive positive change.

I am passionate about helping people step up and lead bigger and more fulfilling lives, but sometimes getting them to realise that they have hidden potential and working with them to unleash that potential can be a challenge – especially if they are struggling to know where to start.

For more than 40 years I have studied human behaviour in different settings and at the very deepest level. In whatever role I was fulfilling as a daughter, a sister, a friend, a wife, a mother, an employee, an employer, a coach, a mentor, a trusted adviser, a consultant, a facilitator or an entrepreneur it taught me that no matter what is going on in your life there is always available room for things to happen that would create much more positivity – just so long as you are willing to notice them, make that space for them and take appropriate actions to get them.

I'm going to share those strategies with you and I've made it so simple you can do it in your coffee break!

During my working life I have worked with and for large global organisations across a broad spectrum of sectors, and having come into contact with many hundreds of thousands of people, has given me the chance to study what distinguishes people who have successful careers and lives from those who do not. I have seen and explored the secrets of those people who are very successful and I want to share their techniques with you here to help you lead the life you would choose to live.

Time and again I have heard clients use the phrase 'crashed and burned' either in describing something that has already happened to them and that proved difficult and they believe has led to an unrecoverable situation or in reference to what they believe would be the outcome if they did a particular something that is outside their comfort zone. Either way, in the particular mindset that they are in and by doing nothing they have remained paralysed and lead ordinary lives.

When I get a sense that clients are stuck or blocked I ask them two questions: "Do you know the phoenix formula?" and "What's really stopping you?" The first question usually gets a "No" response and the second typically gets a reply of, "I honestly don't know."

Whether you believe in it or not I'm sure that you know that the phoenix is a fiery bird of legend, one that is believed to have lived for centuries with the ability to rise from its own funeral pyre with renewed youth and intent to live another cycle. It is the perfect metaphor for individuals who feel stuck or so out of their comfort zone that they withdraw. As a coach my greatest satisfaction is watching clients or people I come into contact with seeing the light bulb come on from just a few questions even though they are feeling at rock bottom and supporting them until they realise that they have so much more they can access, whether it is in themselves or in the external environment, usually by some form of reinvention so that they rise up from their 'ashes' and truly flourish and shine.

The truth about a phoenix is that it is a metaphor for someone who is remarkable in some respect, and that is you.

I know I am a lifelong learner and that I tend to be attracted to working with people who are not willing to settle for average. My clients come to work with me because they are looking for answers/solutions or options to problems or concerns that they are facing that they would not get by simply sticking their head in the sand and hoping things will change by themselves.

This book is designed to be a resource you can turn to whenever you may need it. You will find included stories and case studies from clients I have worked with and I share very honestly the things that worked fastest for them in the hope that if you can relate to the challenges you will get a head start in getting things moving. I am sure the discussions of how circumstances can derail or delay your achievements will resonate with you, but by sharing the coping strategies and positive outcomes I want to give you hope and encouragement that you too can find a way through whatever difficulty or barrier you may have hit.

The tips and strategies I refer to through the text have been specifically chosen because they have worked not just with my clients, but have also worked with me when I have been stuck or at a crossroads.

In my life I have attended more than 200 different courses, each one with the intention of finding an answer to a challenge I was facing at the time. I have spent more than £70,000 attending the events/ seminars/mastermind groups/retreats and if I tried to add up all of the hours/days/weeks of time spent it would probably total four years of consecutive learning over a period of about 20 years. So you see this book is already a bargain; it will save you the time and effort of attendance at many events and won't cost you a fraction of what I have invested.

I also know that many people don't have the luxury of being able to afford a coach but in giving you my best examples and in asking some great questions I am giving you all you need to coach yourself to a place of possibility where magic can happen if you are willing to let it.

After all – what have you got to lose?

So grab a cuppa and let's get cracking.

Chapter 1

EARLIEST MEMORIES

WITH

A LARGE CAFFÈ AMERICANO AND BANANA WALNUT BREAD

We have a lot in common you and I.

We are not just both made of flesh and bones, but we are also both a complex mix of senses, thoughts, feelings, experiences and beliefs.

As a consequence of the experiences you have had it's easy to believe that no one truly understands or gets you.

It's true – I see it in the eyes of the thousands of people I've worked with. Time and again the reaction to my killer question, "Do you feel like a fake?" is a nervous laugh and a response of, "Yes – how did you know?"

If I had a pound or a dollar for everyone who confirms that belief I would be a very rich woman. People of both sexes, but possibly more women, create personas. They wear them like suits of armour regardless of whether they actually need them and when challenged on why they use them (even when they know it doesn't give ample protection); it typically comes back to a fear of being found out.

Business pages in respected journals and newspapers regularly publish pieces about the reasons behind insufficient diversity at board level. Mud gets slung at corporates and governments for not doing enough. However, when I surveyed the FTSE 100 Index (Financial Times Stock Exchange) and the Fortune 500 CEOs and the make up of government ministers the same message came back: The issue in most cases is that the candidates who would create the diversity are just not putting themselves forward to be considered for key roles. In my career I have met and worked with amazing leaders and managers of both sexes, so I know that top talent exists – yet the issues and arguments on diversity and making opportunities available still exist across the globe.

Why?

We are the only people who can make change happen for ourselves. If we don't believe in ourselves or if we are unwilling to put ourselves forward and go out of our comfort zone then we should not be surprised that we don't receive the rewards we think we deserve.

Regardless of gender, somewhere deep inside is likely to reside a belief that you can't do it/will fail/will be found out/will be rejected/will find it too difficult or some other similar version of such a negative message.

Yet, look around you: You will know people in your immediate circle (colleagues, neighbours, friends and relations) who spark a sense of jealousy or envy in you when you compare what they have to your lot in life. How unfair is it that one group of people make it and one group not? Who really decides whether their view of the world is better than the one that you have?

You do.

So who are you? How did you come to be the person reading this book?

It will probably come as no surprise that the answer to these questions goes back to the beginning of your story.

Many psychologists, therapists and coaches on meeting their client for the first time spend some time trying to understand the childhood and early years that that client experienced. So I am going to do exactly the same.

EXERCISE

Sign above the door

This is a quick and interesting technique that I use with lots of my clients. It is useful because it provides clarity and insight without the expenditure of too much effort and energy.

Take a deep breath and clear your mind of everything; you may find it helpful to close your eyes or to just 'zone out' for a few seconds.

I want you to visualise the home that you got taken back to when you were a baby. (I know this may be a challenge, especially if you moved while you were young.)

Imagine that you are standing outside, looking at the front door of that first home. It may not be a totally clear image at first but take a moment to remember as much detail as you can.

As you look up above the door, recognise that there's a sign hanging above it. You will be able to see the words or message really clearly.

What does your sign say?

When it is sketched out for them, many of my clients believe that they will struggle to do this exercise. However, when they do attempt it, they all, without fail, see a message or a group of words.

One female senior manager, who we will call Lara, specifically wanted help in relation to her presence and impact at work. She undertook this exercise with some reluctance, as she was doubtful that it would work for her, particularly as she could not see the relevance of her early years to her current dilemma. Even though her recollection of the house was incredibly vague and woolly, she could relate the words that she saw hanging above the front door: 'Enter at your peril.'

Initially, she was very shocked and unsettled at seeing this message, as she saw her childhood as one that was happy and uneventful. However, as we discussed what those words could mean I saw a light bulb go on as it dawned on Lara exactly why it was that those words had appeared.

Lara had been born into a traditional family. She was the eldest of two children, a girl and a boy. Her mum had given up work after having Lara and like many families in the 1960s her father had become the sole breadwinner. What Lara found most interesting was that her memories of growing up were of being loved but a discussion of what she remembered brought out that she grew up in an environment where there was a sense of undefined sadness.

When Lara was two years old her parents moved to a house in a different town as they wanted to have a larger family home and wanted also to be in a catchment area for better schools. Not long after that her brother was born and Lara became her mother's little helper - a cause of the sadness, as her needs were not being met.

We discussed where in her life right now Lara was repeating the same pattern. She was amazed at what she realised from the analysis. As a grown-up she was particularly focused on relationships, and she would do all that she could to keep her team and her bosses happy – even at her own expense.

Lara recognised that her very earliest experiences taught her patterns that she repeated unconsciously and, as a result, she was seen by some of her bosses as being a lightweight in some situations - pleasing others rather than forming her own opinion.

It is easy to discount a lot about our childhood when we are adults and to assume that it is irrelevant to us in the choices we make.

Like Lara, I also have a brother. I remember having a very typical love/hate relationship with him as we grew up. Sometimes we were co-conspirators against my parents, grandparents or babysitters and sometimes we were running around screaming blue murder at each other. My poor mum. It's only now, as a mother myself and finding myself listening to the endless bickering between my daughters, that I recognise what it must have been like for her and that gives me a greater respect for the challenges she faced.

For some clients it isn't the largely unthought of, general experience, of growing up that may be a key shaper to who they are now but a much more significant experience that is very much in the consciousness but that still goes largely discounted as an influencer on the journey that their life has taken.

EXERCISE

Earliest memory

- What is your earliest memory?

- What value do you place on that memory?

- What do you believe about that memory?

- What do you believe you learned from that situation?

Usually our earliest memory is significant in one way or another for the emotions, values and beliefs that we created in that moment and that we have lived with ever since.

The earliest memory of one of my clients, who we will call Beth, dates to when she was only two and a half years old, which is unusually young.

In relating the memory, Beth painted a very nice picture of a sunny day in early autumn. She could clearly remember playing in a flowery dress in the garden and being quite excited at having a new younger sibling.

The doorbell rang, and on running to see who was at the door she found that it was her beloved grandparents making a surprise visit – which felt like such a treat. Beth told me that she "adored her Granddad" and she created for me a warm vision of a jolly man, large in stature with white hair, twinkly eyes and a very 'naughty laugh'. I was sure that I would have been equally won over.

As her brother was only weeks old, Beth felt that this was probably the reason for the speculative visit. Interestingly, her grandparents didn't have a car and they had used the bus to travel the 20 or so miles (about 32 kilometres) to spend time with their daughter and her family. From Beth's point of view this was such a lovely day – she remembers her granddad chasing her down the garden and spinning her around with her legs flying out while she screamed as only a two and a half year-old could do.

As the day came to an end, Beth's dad offered to drive the grandparents back to their home to save them getting on the bus again – after all it was only about 30 minutes to their house in the car. Fond goodbyes were made and Beth doesn't remember anything in detail after that point.

You may be thinking, "So what?"

Well the point of the story really lies in what happened next.

As far as Beth knows, her dad waved his in-laws off cheerfully as he watched them go up their path and into their house, and he headed back home to his young family.

When she was an adult her dad told her that her grandma went upstairs to hang up her coat and hat and failed to hear a soft thud in the hall. By the time that Beth's dad had arrived back home, not 30 minutes from waving his in-laws off, her granddad had suffered a massive heart attack and had died in the hall.

From Beth's point of view she believes that everything changed from that moment and in discussing it with me she realised that it explained her fear of rejection which she had never considered before.

Beth felt that the family lived in a stormy rain cloud from that day on for a very long time. Her gran moved in with her family and, while she did not remember seeing her mum cry, she knew there was terrible pain and sadness. As a young child she recognised having an overwhelming sense of wanting to make everyone feel all right.

Beth commented that she must have started people-watching at a very young age because she was naturally instinctive in knowing the sort of moods people were in and she would adapt her behaviour to suit. In certain respects these skills had served her very well; as a manager her appraisals at work tell her that she is well liked by her colleagues and that she is highly rated by her teams. However, when Beth's decisions have been challenged she has frequently opted for the safe options rather than having been willing to take risks – even calculated ones – that could have possibly upset or alienated colleagues. She had missed out on two promotions prior to contacting me and believed that a lack of 'killer instinct' was holding her back.

Our early experiences create patterns of behaviour that teach us what works and what will not and whether the option we select is the only or best option often does not get much of a look in in our thinking; we find something that is safe and we stick to it.

My own early experience was starting school. As a baby born in May, I was one of the youngest in my class, and I started school aged four and a bit. My parents had chosen to send me to an all-girls convent where I was taught by a mix of nuns and lay-teachers. I remember the feeling of being afraid that my mum would not come back at the end of the day and I developed separation anxiety. I was sad – and my mum was sad – but the teachers at the school were very cold about how I felt. They had a matter-of-fact way of telling me that my behaviour over the anxiety of being separated was upsetting my mum. As I did not like being told that my behaviour was upsetting, it didn't take me long to learn to not show what I was feeling. Underneath my behaviour was a concern that I would lose my mum, but as a child I could not articulate the emotion. The pattern I developed from this experience was trying to please people and it is something I recognise that I occasionally go back to at different points in my life.

All of my clients talk about the lovely experiences they have had as well, and it is always impressive to hear that many clients are still in touch with early school friends 20 to 30 years later.

Another client, who we will call Andy, remembered being shy and not having many friends before the age of 12. He felt that his peers at the private school he attended were more confident and louder than himself and he remembered feeling in awe and intimidated by the stronger personalities. Academically, Andy was middle of the road, and thus not at the ends of the spectrum normally chosen by those who want to pick on someone, but for whatever reason he became fair game and was bullied for a number of years. I was the first person he ever admitted to that he used to cry about the situation.

He had not wanted to bring the situation to his parents' attention in case they saw him as being weak.

Andy's parents only found out what was going on when another parent mentioned to his mum that their son had said that he was relieved that Andy was in the class otherwise he believed he would have been the one to have been picked on. When Andy's parents spoke to the school they claimed to have no knowledge of the situation. They did speak to the boys involved in the bullying who were made to apologise for their actions in front of the whole school, but Andy never felt that they treated him the same after that. He believed that this experience made him nervous in dealing with conflict and as a result he had found himself in a career that he hated and in a relationship that he knew was going nowhere but feeling paralysed to do anything about either.

I hope by sharing the experiences of my clients you can see that things they experienced in their formative years explained patterns of behaviour or beliefs they held as adults.

Without realising it, our early experiences imprint in our subconscious and because of the fight-or-flight programming human beings have, we all learn our own blueprint to survive that we go back to time and again to help us deal with situations, often without realising it. Psychologists can demonstrate that by the time that we are seven years old most of us will have experienced enough things to have provided us with a framework to cope with situations, be they good, bad or indifferent. We are taught things by the people around us: our parents, our teachers, our siblings and indeed anyone who we interact with. As we grow older, each set of daily experiences we have just layer on top of one another, building confidence, expertise and life experience and while we refine, hone and change our approach depending on the scale of the event that we experience, in general the strategies that we use in our teens, twenties and so forth will just be more refined versions of the things that we learned early on.

In 1:1 coaching sessions I get clients to partake in a number of activities that I'm going to share with you here.

EXERCISE

Timeline

The purpose of this exercise is to think of the period from when you were born to when you turned seven. Try to capture the key events you remember at any stage over that time. It is normal to have no personal recollection of the period from when you were zero to when you were three. However, if you have been told by your parents or by some other way know that your family moved house, or a sibling was born or there were any other significant events then note them down against that age point.

Age

0:

1:

2:

3:

4:

5:

6:

7:

Can you see a relationship between the experiences that you had and the values that you still hold on to now?

A number of clients have told me that they find it difficult to define what their values are. The best definition I have seen is very simple: 'Values are priorities that tell you how to spend your time.'

When I did my own timeline, it showed me that I prioritised:

- wanting to please people and helping them feel good about themselves

- checking out the 'temperature' of other people's mood before making a decision on how I would behave

- not being apart from the people who I love and care about.

Sasha was a client who struggled to sustain a long-term romantic relationship. Using the timeline exercise helped her to remember the benefit to her of learning to read and using a love of stories as a means of escapism from listening to her parents' volatile relationship. She would drown out the shouting and challenges by transporting herself into an adventure. The characters in the books became her friends and she clearly remembered feeling what she described as a sense of grief when she had finished some of the books that had particularly captivated her and she had to leave the storybook characters wherever the book finished. Books also gave her another source of reference, one that made her question her actual life experience. In books, good conquered evil, princes rescued princesses and families lived happy ever after.

As she grew up, Sasha developed wariness about long-term commitment and this affected her life in terms of career and personal relationships. She had developed a pattern where she would move jobs every two to three years and she had never sustained a romantic relationship for more than 18 months. Sasha believed that people would let her down or leave her and because she had never learned skills to cope with this she just did what she could to survive and, as she got older, kept avoiding situations where she might have to find out if people would disappoint her. As a result she was living on nervous energy.

Many clients and colleagues recognise a concept known as 'eggshell syndrome' – this is where we live or operate in an environment where there are high levels of nervous energy, leading to patterns of hyper-vigilant behaviour. These patterns can follow individuals into adulthood, as Sasha found. While she was not in an excessively volatile environment either at work or at home, she continued to look for negative indicators from romantic partners and work colleagues and because that was where her attention was that was all she saw. She recognised that she missed hearing compliments or words of encouragement. So instead of allowing things to grow and develop she walked away anytime that things got difficult. The relief that Sasha felt when she realised the connection between her early experiences and some of the big regrets in her life was massive. In understanding why her life followed this pattern she was able to let go of things that were not going to help her in the future and was able to learn to be OK with past, well-intentioned, decisions.

Part of the reason that 'eggshell syndrome' developed in Sasha's early years was due to her parents' relationship. They believed that their relationship was very passionate and loving at the time. However, when you are small and you are listening to the people that you love screaming at each other, the only feeling you may remember is fear.

Yes, there was making up and nice times as well, but for a lot of the time the atmosphere was tense and fraught and Sasha, like so many other clients come to realise, adapted her behaviour based on how she judged the situation she was faced with to try to 'fix' things.

Clients who have felt lonely or who are socially awkward remember that they did not have many friends at school, as there were often things that they wanted to keep secret about their home life and not draw to anyone's attention. The sad thing about that situation is that they didn't have anyone to talk to about what was going on. They didn't learn how to trust people, a situation that inevitably holds them back in many relationship areas.

A different client, who we will call Pippa, recognised that a difficult experience in her early teens actually played an important part in helping her become more socially confident. From the age of five to the age of 10 her parents paid for her to go to a private school, which she knew cost a lot of money, and she was always being told of the sacrifice that everyone was making to give her that opportunity. As happens to children all around the world, she was bullied by a group of older girls because of her physical appearance, in her particular case because of her tiny frame and the fact that she wore glasses on and off for two years.

If she had not been repeatedly told how much her parents were giving up in order to allow her to have the benefit of private education she may have felt able to tell them of how unhappy she was. As it was, she kept those feelings completely to herself. When she had just turned 11 her parents found themselves financially stretched after a business deal went wrong and they took her out of private school.

Pippa's parents could not understand why Pippa was so happy about leaving her private school and when she explained what had been going on they were initially angry with her and then expressed deep guilt that she had not felt able to talk to them truthfully about her experiences. If her parents had been aware of what was going on then they would have been able to take action to help her.

One of the positives about moving school, however, was that it allowed Pippa to recreate herself without any baggage. Being a new girl joining a school aged 12 definitely gave her an air of mystery and so other students were fighting over being her buddy and wanting the kudos of being the 'new girl's friend'. Pippa remembered that in being excluded by the girls at her old school she had become used to being on her own and in being in a new environment she had to force herself to join in rather than being her usual shy, lonely self.

I could relate to a lot of this experience. I changed schools at 14 when my dad's business got into difficulty. I had mixed experiences with different friendship groups – some good and some not so good – and while I was scared of the new environment I was willing to give it my best shot and see what would happen if I behaved in a different way. Not all of the girls were friendly as some believed that I wasn't 'cool' enough for them, but on many levels the change in environment was brilliant in as much as that I did make some truly wonderful friends that supported me through thick and thin and who are still my friends today, 30 years later.

If you are still feeling that there is not enough context coming to mind yet to help you explain or make sense of your thoughts or beliefs about certain situations then here are some questions that are designed to be asked and answered really quickly so that you don't have time to overthink the answers. Just go with your gut response.

The quiz about you

My earliest memory is

....

....

....

....

....

Being a child felt:

....

....

....

....

I would describe my family as:

....

....

....

....

My greatest role model was:

....

....

....

....

My biggest challenge as a child was:

....

....

....

....

Primary/Junior school was:

....

....

....

High/Secondary school was:

....

....

....

My friends taught me:

....

....

....

My happiest moment was:

....

....

....

When I was sad I:

....

....

....

When I was happy I:

....

....

....

....

If I could change one thing about this time in my life it would be:

....

....

....

....

SUMMARY

Being able to understand your early years and the values and beliefs you created during that time will explain so much about the decisions and options you have taken in your adult life. Yet it is something we typically spend very little time reflecting on and thinking about, especially if it was an unhappy time.

By realising and accepting that in the intervening years you have done the best you could do with everything that was available to you will I hope allow you to give yourself some credit and at the same time lay some ghosts to rest.

Time and again my clients are amazed as to how much clarity they can achieve just by drawing links between their early memories and what is keeping them stuck or stopping them from moving on or taking a different approach in life now. Once they have this insight they are often able to consider where other experiences are possibly blocking them from being more successful/happy/healthy or whatever it is they wish for themselves.

Chapter 2

THINGS THAT SHAPE US

WITH

AN ICED SKINNY FLAVOURED LATTE AND A CHEWY CHOCOLATE MERINGUE COOKIE

There is no getting away from it: There are two absolute certainties in life – death and taxes. So it should come as no surprise that in your life any experience of losing someone or something will have shaped who you are today.

I have many clients who – like Beth, discussed in the previous chapter – have as part of their earliest memories the death of a close family member or the death of a pet.

Even though she was only two and a half years old when it happened, Beth vividly remembers the last day that she saw her granddad because when he was dropped home that day he died suddenly. She recognised that she did not fully appreciate what had happened, as she was so young. She knew that after her lovely day playing together she never saw him again and that her house became very sad, but she had not realised that the two things were connected.

Nor had Beth recognised that her fear of rejection and loss could be seeded in this early situation and that in wanting to avoid such feelings in later life she had frequently been unwilling to take risks and had discounted many opportunities that had been presented to her.

As with any new event, it is only as we experience things and reflect on the possible learning that any of this makes sense.

A senior manager I was working with, who we will call Felix, remembered a death of a pet when he was a child having an impact on him. As most children do, Felix wore his parents down into letting him have his first pet. Initially, he had wanted a snake; the school that his parents sent him to owned a number of interesting reptiles that pupils could look after in the holidays and he thought that owning something like a snake would be very cool. Naturally, Felix's parents were far less sure about having a snake for a pet and he recognised later that his mum had probably actually been terrified at the thought of such a daunting prospect – imagining scenarios of the snake escaping and so forth.

Felix described himself as an average student, with a few good friends, who wanted to 'fit in' socially while also liking the idea of doing something risky and different. The same applies today.

While Felix had no concept at the time of cost or what else was involved in purchasing or owning a snake and had little understanding of why he was told no, he admitted that he sulked and stropped in the hope that he could bring about a change of heart from his parents by being so horrible. They did not budge.

One day Felix saw an advert outside a house that said: 'Rabbits for Sale'. While he did not expect his parents to answer in the affirmative he requested the purchase of one in order to be contrary. He clearly remembered the surprise and elation he felt when, having expected the usual "No", his dad came home from work the following Friday with a box that contained a black and white rabbit for him.

Snoopy, as he was named, was black all over except for one white paw and a white circle around one eye. He was also totally mad. Whenever he was let out to play in the garden he would bounce up and down on the grass, occasionally leaping exceptionally high and flicking his back legs out.

Felix laughingly recounted how Snoopy learned how to chew his way out of his chicken wire door so he could try to get amorous with the female rabbit that lived in the next-door garden, much to the understandable annoyance of Felix's neighbours, as Snoopy would chew his way into that rabbit's hutch.

Eventually his luck ran out, and on one such escapade Snoopy must have met a fox on his travels across the boundary and Felix's poor dad was met with a rather gruesome sight early one morning.

Having nagged for his pet, Felix conceded that he was probably quite selfish in that he was only willing to give his rabbit attention when it suited him. There were numerous occasions when his mum would shout at him to clean out Snoopy's hutch or change the water in his water bottle and like a typical teenager he would rebel and do the jobs when he wanted to do them.

In losing him in such a tragic way, Felix remembered feeling two different emotions: distress at not having him in his life any more and at having lost a creature he cared about but also some relief at not having to have responsibility any more for something that had been a chore.

This dual sense of sadness and relief is quite a normal reaction and can show up in other situations when things come to an end, especially if the situation has been uncomfortable. Where a loss occurs unexpectedly it can be harder to come to terms with or to make sense of what is going on and how to deal with it.

I remember watching a Disney film, *The Lion King*, when my daughters were young and seeing them get so upset when the father was killed and then explaining to them that we all go on a similar journey was a vital lesson to understand and learn in order that they would notice and appreciate so many more good things that they would have otherwise discounted as being unimportant.

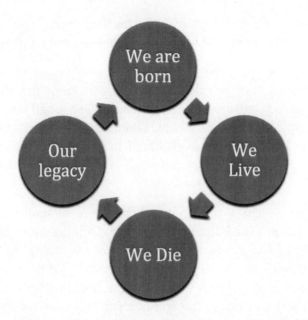

Sometimes the loss that we have to deal with is not all that we can or are meant to take away from a situation. I learned that for myself when I was only 14. As I have already mentioned, I changed schools and I benefited from the chance to reinvent myself. In a slightly warped way I missed some of the familiarity of my old school; I missed seeing the teachers and the children who I had known since I was four. However, I enjoyed what the new school was able to offer and I was able to show that I was not the same weak girl that had been picked on and that had been written off by some of the staff.

Sports Day is usually a great event in a schools calendar. It is a chance to show off individual and team athletic talents as well as an opportunity for parents, past pupils and potential future students to come and see what is going on. I managed to convince my parents to take me out of my new school for that one day and take me back to my old school so I could see and be seen.

I remember having a great day and it was nice to see so many people I knew and who knew me. I felt appreciated in ways I never had when I had been a pupil at the school. People commented on how grown up I seemed and I felt that I had made my parents proud. I believed when I went home that night that I had laid some ghosts to rest.

On returning to my new school the following day with renewed vigour, I expected everyone to be very excited as it was the last day before breaking up for the summer holidays – another reason I'd been able to convince my parents to let me take the day off, as it was so close to the end of term. However, instead I was very confused to find teachers talking in hushed voices in the school corridor and the girls in my class being in tears. Finally, one of my friends explained that a girl in my class, Angela, had fallen ill and had been collected by her dad the day before. They believed that she was very poorly and that she was in hospital. By lunchtime our class had been called together and the deputy headmistress talked to us in a very gentle voice, updating us on Angela's progress. She had been diagnosed by then with meningitis and as a precaution we were all being issued with a course of antibiotics and we were each being given a letter for our parents explaining the situation.

Even though I'd only known Angela for about 10 months she had been very kind to me. She was a boarder at the school as her dad worked for the RAF and while the day-girls and boarders mixed during class time, naturally the boarders had a very close bond and typically kept to themselves at recreational times – although, unusually, the day before Angela had fallen ill we had played tennis together and had the longest chat we had ever had from the time of me joining.

I remember going home as school broke up, with the little bottle of antibiotics and the letter for my parents, thinking what a lousy start it was to the summer holiday for Angela and deciding to write her a letter telling her about my day seeing my old friends. You see I had confided in her when we had played tennis about taking the following day off and what I was really going to be doing when I would not be in school. She had thought that I would get into trouble but had promised that she would not tell anyone where I was. We had also swapped general chitchat about what our plans were for the summer.

In the days before emails and mobiles to communicate at a distance you had to sit down and write a letter. I churned out four or five pages of waffle and chat all intended to make her smile. I also decided to enclose in the envelope loads of rubbish random photos I had taken in the hope that it may cheer her up – there were, after all, no digital cameras in those days either. I popped my letter in the post to her home address expecting to get a reply at some time over the summer. It was Thursday night.

At 15 you are almost an adult – don't you agree? The need for independence at this age is great and for me having money equated to being independent so I had found a weekend job to earn myself some pocket money. It was working in a designer boutique, which my mum loved as one of the perks was that she got all of the clothes that she wanted at half price and consequently she did not mind getting up to drive me the 15 or so miles to work each Saturday and Sunday.

A number of my new school friends would pop their heads in from time to time to see me and say hello, so it was no surprise when one of them popped in that Saturday after we had broken up. When I asked if she had any news of Angela she nodded. "How's she doing?" I asked. When the reply was that she was not very good I immediately felt a bit sick. You see this particular girl's brother had been Angela's first boyfriend so I knew that she would be in the know.

"Angela died this morning ..."

I was completely stunned. All I could think of was my letter, in the post, winging its way to her house and how stupid I was for writing so much rubbish and how awful and tacky it would come over to her grieving parents.

I genuinely couldn't get my head around how someone who was only 15 could die from what had started off as a cold. We are supposed to be indestructible aren't we at that age. I finished work that day and cried for hours, partly for the loss of my friend, partly from feeling embarrassed about my letter and partly because of feelings of guilt because I'd taken a day off school and if only I hadn't then maybe she wouldn't have fallen ill.

Because it was the summer holiday there was no need to get up the following morning. On the Tuesday morning the house phone rang and I could hear my dad in conversation with someone. After five minutes or so he came into my room and told me that it was Angela's dad on the phone and he wanted to talk to me. A hot flush washed over me; I wasn't sure if he was going to tell me off or be nice. Either way, I had absolutely no idea what to say to him. I took the phone with a little trepidation.

I needn't have worried; he was so lovely and graceful at a time that his heart must have been breaking. He thanked me so genuinely for my funny letter and for the photos and assured me that Angela would have loved to have received it. He explained that by the time he got her to hospital on the Wednesday she was very ill and while the doctors had done everything they could, she had been too poorly to survive. He took so much time in trying to make me feel better and to reassure me that my letter hadn't upset them at all. In fact, he related, it had apparently given them much comfort in knowing that Angela was so loved that a friend would take the time to immediately write to her wishing her well. He told me that there would be a memorial at the start of term and said that he looked forward to meeting me in person then.

I was always so grateful for that call and in fact over a number of years following I kept in touch with her parents. They were very keen to hear about Angela's friends, as it allowed them to keep that link going.

As a parent now I realise what an enormous effort and sacrifice her parents made in ensuring that they reassured her friends that it was OK to grieve. They put their need to shed tears to one side and instead they wrapped their arms around us as we sobbed on their shoulders. Maybe in some small way helping us helped them. At the memorial service they gave us photographs and keepsakes of Angela, some of which I still have today. I learned so much from the way that Angela's parents conducted themselves at this time. They turned their pain into so much positive energy. I know that I used that same technique myself in the years that followed and I have encouraged many clients to take their grief and pain and turn it to their advantage, too – even when it's the last thing they feel like doing.

I have worked with many clients who, because of the nature of the loss they have suffered, feel paralysed and so distressed that they cannot imagine being able to move forward. They do not necessarily see that they create a cycle where they continually relive the pain and keep the sense of loss fresh.

Working together we discuss what is it that they feel they need to hold on to – for some it is a sense of unfinished business, especially if the situation was outside of their control; for others it has become a habit and they need to break the pattern. The thing that they all have in common is not having the ability to channel the negative energy into something positive.

Another huge lesson in loss happened to another client – Tony – who had failed a promotion panel and who had 'lost it' in the office in front of colleagues. One of the questions I asked him when we first met was whether he could remember a time that he wished he had behaved differently. This was his story.

Tony was about 23 years old when I knew him and he was less than worldly wise. At the time he was working as an HR officer for a global engineering company, something that was a little unusual, as most of his colleagues in HR were female. There were about 300 employees working in Tony's office and because of the nature of his role he felt that he knew the staff very well. Late one morning one of the senior managers came into Tony's office, closed the door, looked straight at Tony, and said, "There's no easy way to say this but one of my team has had a bereavement – his little girl died in the night. She was only 9 months old."

Tony remembered organising a donation on behalf of the staff for the cot death charity and sending a card to the bereaved family. However, the reason he felt that this memory demonstrated a time when he wished he had done something different was in relation to how he treated the grieving staff member when that gentleman returned to work.

Tony shared, ashamedly, that because he was young and had no idea what to say or how to behave around this person because of what he had experienced, he said nothing to him and went out of his way to limit contact or to just behave like nothing significant had happened. In Tony's defence, he believed that his intention was to not cause any additional distress to the employee.

Nine months or so later my client ended up sitting next to the grieving father at a staff social and casually asked, "How are you doing?"

Initially, the guy responded quite coolly, saying, "How do you think?"

Tony related to me that he remembered wishing that the ground could have opened up and swallowed him right then and there, but what happened next surprised and humbled him. His bereaved colleague began to explain that he understood why people felt unable to reach out to him but that those first weeks back at work were almost as terrible as dealing with the death of his daughter itself. As people weren't talking to him, he felt uncomfortable engaging with them, and he felt very isolated. He explained that in that situation he would have preferred it if people had said completely the wrong thing rather than not saying anything. He knew that people cared because of the card and the large amount of money raised but if only Tony and others had reached out to him, even in their clumsiest way, it would have made those early weeks trying to find normality a little easier.

Again, I have worked with clients who have similar stories where they have regretted their behaviour and it has held them back – primarily in putting themselves forward for better things. A number believe that they are unable to deal with people and have therefore sidestepped opportunities to manage teams and have virtually sent their career down a cul-de-sac as they have been leapfrogged by colleagues who have been willing to take on that challenge and who, in doing so, are given more and/or greater responsibilities.

The amazing thing about Tony's colleague was that he forgave people for their clumsiness and unintentional lack of support because he knew that behind it was a fear of making the situation worse.

Some clients get angry talking about friends and colleagues failing to support them at difficult times and they build the frustration up into a big wall of anger and, in extreme cases, mistrust.

Hundreds of relationships have broken down because of this very human failing, yet when the red mist settles in our sessions and I get the clients to take a deep breath and be willing to see what may have been going on, then in almost all cases my clients are willing to see that the reason they were "let down" was a consequence of friends/colleagues/relations feeling so out of their depth in knowing the right way to support them that they have either withdrawn or ignored the issue. Then the client can decide whether to hold on to the anger or hurt or whatever the negative emotions are or find a way to forgive and move on.

Interestingly, I have faced similar difficult and uncomfortable situations in my own life and I have learned that saying or doing something with the right intention, even if what it was was clumsily delivered or was in some other way awkward and caused some initial upset, was better in the long run than saying nothing. Being responsible for my behaviour meant that I was able to help support, empathise and encourage whoever was in pain and they were grateful for my attempts at condolence or similar. I was always grateful myself for support, even when it was clumsy.

What occasions do you wish you could return to and behave differently at? Or can you think of ones that were uncomfortable, where you felt tongue-tied or where you struggled to make eye contact with someone, not because you didn't care but because you felt helpless and embarrassed?

Have you ever experienced an event where you needed people's support and yet you found yourself treated as an outcast and came away incredibly hurt? Could it have been that the people you expected to spring into action felt so helpless and uncertain of what to say to help you that they chose to say nothing? Do you still hold it against any of them if they are still in your life?

Loss can show up in lots of different guises – being made redundant, falling out with a close friend or family member or breaking up with a loved one. The feelings of anger, loss, vulnerability and confusion usually apply across the spectrum.

Many clients I have worked with as part of an outplacement package talk about being hurt by the behaviour of former colleagues, especially when they disappear overnight. One director I knew, called Bob, was called to a normal meeting with the managing director one evening only to find the HR director sat alongside them and the conversation turning into, "It's not you, it's me," and Bob being given a compromise agreement to sign. He had to clear his office the same night. For his colleagues it was as if he had died suddenly. Bob was stunned to see the business kept going without his input. When Bob saw people out and about, he noticed that they were reluctant to make eye contact and for a while he felt like he had something contagious that others did not want to catch.

Other clients have worked in businesses that have gone into receivership. They tend to talk about the close connection they feel to old colleagues because they all went through the experience together. It's also natural to look back and view some experiences through rose-coloured glasses even if they were not that good at the time.

All of these reactions can be explained and are completely normal, but where clients have not been willing to let go or have not been willing to see another version of what may have been going on they have stayed stuck. Everyone experiences grief at different rates, and if it was illustrated as a curve it would vary in depth, length and width. Some people find ways to move quicker than others. The truth is that only you will truly know when you are willing to let something go.

EXERCISE

When my clients are affected by a loss we explore together the following questions:

- What was the loss?

- When did it happen?

- What would it feel like if you could let it go?

- How is it serving you by holding on to it?

- What are the bad things that will happen if you do let it go?

- What are the good things that will happen if you let it go?

- Where else in your life are you following the same pattern?

- What are you teaching your children/colleagues/family by holding on to this?

Write down three things you can do to help yourself at difficult times. (Then whenever you need them they should come into your mind really quickly.)

....

....

....

....

....

....

....

....

....

....

....

....

SUMMARY

Loss comes in all shapes and sizes. It is frequently a painful experience and can dent confidence and self-esteem. However, it is something that we have the ability to cope with. None of my clients enjoyed the experiences that they had but what they recognised was if they had not had them then they would not have been the people they were at the point of working with me and all of them had positive things in their life even with the loss being part of their makeup.

Clients who have been stuck or dissatisfied because of a loss or slight they have experienced found that using the exercise above helped them take steps to move on and upwards.

CHANGING YOUR THINKING

WITH

A SMALL HOT CHOCOLATE AND A CARROT CAKE MUFFIN WITH PECANS

Have you ever had a thought?

Chances are the answer is yes. However, have you ever consciously noticed what the type of thought did to your energy or your motivation?

One thing I learned on many of the courses I've attended over the years is that a lot of what and how you experience things and situations is down to your mindset. When clients shared their thoughts on things they believed were difficult issues or features of things that they saw as barriers I enabled them to make huge progress if I could get them to reframe their thinking about the topic.

When I was training in neurolinguistic programming (NLP) in my early career we were taught that, unwittingly, people's speech patterns can send commands or instructions to our brain that we then agree with or follow. For example, if someone introduces a story or activity by saying something negative such as, "This will be difficult/hard/painful…" then they are laying the bait for you to be looking for the difficulty/pain and that is the element that you will probably notice. Whereas if they had said, "This will be fun/exciting/inspired…" then you would be tuned in to look for those feelings and will therefore have a different experience.

With the latter, even if there are some tricky bits included you will see them through different eyes.

EXERCISE

Have you ever written a list of all the positive and negative experiences you have ever had?

Just for a minute, write down as many things as you can remember in both categories.

Positive things I can remember:

....

....

....

....

....

Negative things I can remember:

....

....

....

....

....

How many things came to mind?

For which category was it easier to recall things?

Here is how one client decided to take what was a potentially negative experience and turn it in to a positive one.

Becca came to me because she was struggling with a lack of confidence and it was affecting how her bosses saw her. In the previous year she had turned 40, her divorce had been finalised signalling the end of 17 years of marriage and she found herself a single mum to two young children. She had struggled going from being part of a long-standing couple to being on her own and the thought of two big milestones occurring so close together had made her feel very anxious in the preceding year – but Becca had kept that to herself.

Perhaps if you have been through such an experience you will empathise with the pain, vulnerability and angst this caused. Now Becca could have chosen to wallow in pity and let the impending events consume and mar the year that she would be turning 40 (an event that after all should be a celebration). However, what I learned during our coaching sessions that occurred after the events of that year was that she consciously decided that in order to raise her game and behave like a survivor she needed to find a way to turn what she feared would be a difficult and negative experience into something positive.

Becca's positive plan was that from 31 December of the preceding year until 31 December of the year she turned 40 she would strive to enjoy/create/experience '40 New First Things' and that getting her 'first' divorce would be just one of them.

I was impressed at her ingenuity and recognised that in setting this goal she was hoping to create a positive energy for the 12 months she would work on this plan. Over three different sessions together she shared the ups and the downs of her year.

I could understand why Becca's list became quite a talking point with her friends. She admitted that many thought that she was completely bonkers for giving herself such a stressful challenge but she did not really listen to their concerns for her. She was working full-time at this point in a role that was incredibly challenging and she was a mum to two girls who were still very young (only five and seven) and who were still needing a lot from their mum. The sorts of things she put on her list were sports-related – learning to ski, learning to horse ride, going to a Premiership football match and watching a cricket match at Edgbaston Cricket Ground (in Birmingham) – as well as such things as new places to visit and bands to see. Her girls went to their father every other weekend so she crammed stuff in on the weekends that she was free but also went all out to create new experiences that included her girls on the weekends that she had them.

When we discussed what was probably the truth about why she had created this ambitious plan Becca conceded that while her intention was to survive the year and not have it defined just by getting divorced and turning 40, she realised she had created a plan that meant it was possible to run away from dealing with the feelings that come with a marriage breaking down and how she felt about the change in her circumstances and what having her age start with a '4' really meant.

Some firsts were sad: She had to have a much loved cat put down because he became very ill and then had to help her daughters learn how to cope with that bereavement.

Some firsts were painful: Becca learned to ski in a day at a local skiing centre prior to going on a first skiing holiday. As many novice skiers do, she fell over early on the first day of training and to break her fall splayed the thumb and fingers of her right hand in the snow to try to anchor herself. She said that she remembered feeling a pull but as she could move everything afterwards she didn't think any more about it. Four months later, when it was still painful, and when she noticed difficulty in writing and opening jars and bottles with her right hand, she decided to seek medical help. Laughingly, she said she was duly chastised for not seeking help at the time of the accident and having reported for an X-ray was shown a lovely picture of the pieces of bone floating free in her hand. As Becca had never broken a bone or been in a plaster cast previously, she just added it to her growing list of firsts.

Some firsts were naughty: She had a brief fling with a chap who on finding out that she had never made love under the stars thought that that was a first he could help her with. She had had her legs waxed for years but one of the things she'd never tried was a Brazilian wax – ouch.

Some firsts were fun: Becca took her daughters on their first camping holiday and went to a couple of music festivals so that she could 'get down with the kids'. On the day of her 40th birthday one of her best friends hired a hot tub and arranged for it to be delivered and set up in her garden – with a bit of help from her mum. She was completely overwhelmed.

As the year wore on, Becca was getting closer to the magic 40 things. She admitted that by the October she was pretty tired – more tired than she knew. Her job was tough and another difficult first she had realised was that her HR director was bullying her. When I asked her why she did nothing to challenge this, she explained that she was not alone; in the time that she had worked for the company this particular HR director had driven a number of people to breakdown but because of fear no one was willing to make a complaint. Becca believed that she was strong enough to deal with the intermittent barrage of insulting and undermining comments and thus battled on.

As the year drew to a close she was driving the 60 or so miles (97 kilometres) into work in tears and ashamedly she admitted that the nearer she got to work the more she felt sick. You see she too was experiencing the 'eggshell syndrome' I have already mentioned. As Becca pulled into the multi-storey car park there were times she thought about throwing herself off. She went on to explain to me that the thing that always stopped her doing anything desperate was the love for her daughters and the fact that she didn't want to cause anyone any mess. I noticed her shock at actually articulating the pain she was in but that in putting it into words and putting it out into the world she stopped it having such a hold on her.

Looking back, Becca reflected it probably was not a surprise that on 18 December she achieved her 40th first milestone – however, it wasn't in the way she had intended. She had her first and hopefully her last nervous breakdown.

During a number of sessions we explored what had stopped her asking for help – it came back to believing that it would have been seen as a sign of weakness and because of her ex-husband being unfaithful Becca was sure that she would be rejected. Yet when I tested the truth in this belief she remembered times that she had asked for help and could recall her friends being only too willing to give their support. You see the capable, in control, confident person Becca projected to the outside world was a sham and by filling her time to capacity on the weekends that she didn't have her daughters it stopped her noticing how lonely and in need of support she was.

Becca realised through some painful but courageous reflection that because she didn't value or appreciate herself very much it was no surprise that other people treated her badly.

Her light bulb moment in coaching was when she realised that she had never stopped to think about who she was after her separation or what she now wanted and how she could get there.

Many people, both men and women, do exactly the same when a relationship comes to an end – they carry on on autopilot too afraid to find out who they now are and what they now want. Yet, by not taking the time to evaluate where you are and what you want, the chances are that you will miss seeing opportunities that can help you get where you want to be.

One of the tools Becca found really helpful to use to get clear what she wanted in the future was 'The Wheel of Life'.

'The Wheel of Life' is a circle split into whatever you believe to be the main categories that your life divides into. An example is shown below.

What I got Becca to do first was to rate each area on of a scale of zero to 10 on how happy or satisfied she was right now with that aspect. Then I asked her to give herself a score of zero to 10 on what she wanted it to be. For some things she was pleased to find that she was already pretty close to having them exactly as she wanted them. For others, there was a gap. What we discussed was what she needed to do differently to get the gap to close and then we explored how she would make it happen.

Over a number of months we continually reviewed the plan and tweaked or revised parts as necessary. One of the lessons Becca learned was that making time for herself was actually an important target to aim for. She also had to consider what she was teaching her daughters in behaving in the ways that she did.

EXERCISE

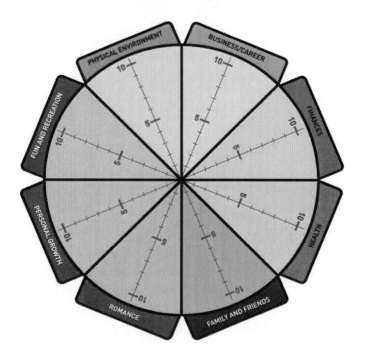

Using the wheel of life above, rate each segment based on where you are right now – score yourself on how you feel about each of the areas of the circle giving a score out of 10 for how happy/satisfied you feel with it.

0 = really unhappy/dissatisfied;
10 = really happy/satisfied

Then think about each of the areas again and decide what you would like the scores to be, giving 0 if the area is not important to you up to 10 if the area is very important to you.

Note that you do not have to give 10/10 to everything.

The reason that there is a different emphasis in the question is because you are trying to find out if you are spending your time on what makes you happy. Many hundreds of my clients have found that the things they would love to spend their time on are the things that get overlooked or pushed to the side and they are spending their time on stuff they either don't enjoy or don't need to do.

One of the most important things with this task is to review honestly and be kind to yourself regardless of where you come out.

Depending on how old you are, there may be certain things that you just have not had chance to experience yet. In having expectations of events and activities you may need to set realistic timescales.

The great thing about this exercise is that you can review and tweak it regularly, so as your situation changes you can think about what and where you want to be focusing your time and effort.

SUMMARY

Thinking can be a dangerous pastime, especially if we over-think or over-analyse situations. Not thinking things through can also lead to pain, however. The art of being able to find a good balance is crucial to having a happy life. Noticing and accepting that a thought is just a thought and it will come and go or change is an important skill to learn. Being aware of what is going on in the different aspects of our life is also important simply because without being aware of how we are doing means that we cannot make tweaks or changes to improve things. The great news I can share is that Becca mentioned in this chapter made a full recovery from her breakdown and is living a much more fulfilled and happy life.

Chapter 4

SHOWING UP

WITH

ORANGE AND MANGO SMOOTHIE WITH A FETA AND SPINACH WRAP

Whether we realise it or not we all create an impression or imprint on the people around us – every action we take or every activity we are part of means we send out and receive messages from a variety of sources.

People who spend time with us in person or observing us from afar will get used to our mannerisms, our energy levels, our use of language and the clothes that we wear and this pattern becomes the 'normal version' of us, a bit like our default setting. If any of our 'normal' behaviour changes people in our closest circle around us would notice first.

There are times when the behaviour changes are positive: We may learn a new skill or have a new experience, which exhilarates us. We won't be able to help ourselves: We will just shine a bit brighter naturally, even if we try to appear as normal as possible.

There will also be times when things aren't going well for us: We may be feeling ill/have had bad news/experienced a disappointment/lost something that was important to us/made a mistake/incurred a cost.

Now what is interesting is that in these sets of circumstances we may be more conscious of how we behave around others. So it may be possible to fool people into believing that things are completely fine and for them to be unaware of any challenges in our lives. However, those that know us best will probably spot changes. The difficulty for them is when they ask if everything is OK and they are told, "Everything is fine." They will believe that they misread the signals and messages they are receiving from us. If this pattern gets repeated a lot people around us will begin to doubt their understanding of our 'default setting' and may not reach out to us when we are in need of support but are unwilling to ask for it.

One in three of us at some point are likely to experience some sort of emotional crisis in our lives and over the years I have seen and worked with many clients either when they are in the middle of their crisis or after it has happened.

In a small number of cases those clients have been supported at a session with a friend, family member or colleague and in nearly every one of those particular cases it came as a complete shock for the other party, because the person experiencing the pain or feelings of being overwhelmed hid it for a very long time and others around them reset the default setting accordingly.

Like Becca in chapter 3, some individuals believe that they have to keep their feelings very private and should only behave and show up as the version that others expect to see; there is a fear of rejection or being considered weak or a failure – even when the truth is very different.

Are you guilty of that?

The first step to recovery, which is often a difficult truth to accept, is helping the client to accept that it was their behaviour and the way they showed up that created the space for them to get into such a bad place.

Whether it was a conscious or unconscious decision, they have worn a mask, just like an actor or actress taking on a role, and somewhere in their subconscious they have created a plausible legend so that the motivation, body language and so forth that fits the character they have created is seen and believed by the people around them.

I have talked specifically about this topic to audiences and when I ask if anyone can relate to the 'character-creation process', 90% of the faces looking at me nod back. In some instances following the talk people come up to me, sometimes in tears, because the truth in my words has hit home hard.

I worked with a young engineering manager – Simon – who felt so trapped in a career that he didn't enjoy that it drove him to become an alcoholic. It did not seem that odd to his colleagues that Simon always had a coke bottle on his desk or that he carried a coke bottle to meetings with him – what many of them never knew was that the coke was laced with vodka and that the only way he believed he could function was if he knew that he had ready access to alcohol all day.

For years and years Simon showed up and managed to be productive and effective, but eventually the effort of being something that he wasn't became too much: His boss began to notice erratic behaviour on a number of different occasions. His boss checked directly with Simon if things were OK and was given plausible explanations for his behaviour, but he followed through with his hunch and asked the HR team to provide some support.

There is no doubt that Simon was incredibly fortunate to work for an organisation that had policies and processes in place to support employees dealing with alcohol dependency. Part of that support meant that he was offered some coaching to help him understand what had happened and how he could change his behaviour to stop himself going back to the place that had driven him to drink. He made one slip at the start of the 12-step programme that he was offered, but he eventually made a full recovery. Because he knew that part of the problem was trying to be an engineer – a career that, on probing, turned out to be the one his father and grandfather had both had, we did some career coaching and identified possible roles he could still do in the company but that were his choice. Very fortunately, the gap between what he had been doing and what he could go on to do only required some training in different types of computer software available on the market, which his company were happy to fund and, within three months he returned to work in a new role and as a completely different person.

As far as I know Simon is now a director in the same organisation and in the years since his 'unmasking' he has been an outstanding role model in supporting and assisting colleagues who are not doing so well and in encouraging people to be the honest version of themselves.

I have never yet met anyone who has been deliberately trying to mislead anyone or behave in a fake way maliciously, but on discovering a possible gap between who they think they really are and who they show up being, there is usually an underlying belief that if they had showed up and behaved in the way that was more genuine to how they were feeling then friends, family, colleagues and so forth would not want to associate with them.

Yet when I ask my audience what evidence they can share with me that specifically proves this belief to be true, they very rarely can think of anything.

All of us, at some point, will show up and flex or stretch our behaviour to meet what our colleagues or family members may be expecting regardless of whether we recognise that version we present as being the authentic version of ourselves.

And it is from this place in our minds that we create our own internal myth about being a fake. If that is true for you, do you worry that you will be 'found out'?

But why do we do it? After all, no one tells us to be that way. I know that there are many theoretic models that try to explain it, but here's one that I like to use with my clients for its three-step simplicity.

Step one: We have a thought.

Step two: This thought creates a feeling inside of us.

Step –three: That feeling creates an external behaviour.

Repeat the cycle endlessly.

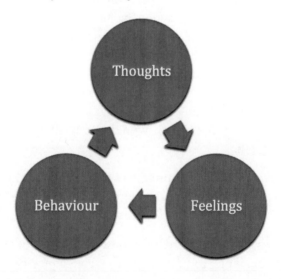

Typically without realising it, as we go through life we create a persona – an image that is a mix of role play and misunderstood belief and that is contextualised for the people we are with, what we are doing and where we are in our lives. We create a story for people about ourselves composed of bits of information that we are willing to share or acknowledge and from it comes plots and sub-plots and decisions regarding relationships, purchases, careers, travel, finances and so forth.

Our image sends out messages from our behaviour depending on the context of social/professional/home life that people see us in. For example, another client, who we will call Emma, was married to a man who frequently said to her that he couldn't understand how she had a responsible job making decisions and dealing with senior directors when she was so vague, weak and indecisive at home. Emma was a senior manager in a global organisation managing a team of people across the UK. As her husband had labelled and defined her at-home behaviour, she believed that that was how she needed to behave at home and, therefore, much to her embarrassment, conceded that she probably did behave in a weak, vague and indecisive manner at home unnecessarily.

Yet at work people would have been horrified to know that Emma held that view of herself, as, five days a week, they saw a happy, confident, decisive, in-control person, someone that they trusted to help them make important business decisions.

When I asked Emma which version of herself made her feel the happiest, it was clearly easy for her to give an answer – she felt more authentic being the strong, confident, in-control person and disliked the other version of herself. On exploring what was the trigger that enabled the switch to occur, Emma concluded that it was down to how she interpreted her husband's communication style – which she described as being negative, controlling and bullying, as he would use mind games with her in order to maintain control in the relationship. Because Emma showed up in two different places in two extreme versions of herself she felt that she was living a massive lie and was continually fearful of being 'found out'. This affected her confidence and self-esteem, which yo-yoed depending where and whom she was with.

There was also a third dimension to Emma's persona, which was the version that her friends saw. They saw a happy, carefree woman who had the ideal life, and Emma laughingly told me of how her friends would comment that they were a bit jealous of what she had as, in the company of others, her husband seemed very supportive and caring.

Trying to be something that you're not is unsustainable in the long run and after a number of years of living this way Emma decided that she had to break free. She brought the marriage to an end. Her friends and family admitted after the event that they had heard her husband make derogatory remarks to her but as she always responded in good humour they had generally missed the nasty undertone. Her response had deflected their attention from the situation, and they were genuinely shocked, upset and angry to find out what life had really been like.

The anger came from the fact that Emma showed up in a way that implied that all was well, when in fact it wasn't, and her friends and family felt cheated as they were unable to help her escape much earlier from her unhappy life.

Does any of this resonate with you?

Are there areas of your life where you show up as someone else's version of yourself?

What would you need to have happen to allow you to be the authentic version of you?

Is there anyone you know who may be living this pattern?

What would you be willing to do to help them?

One of the things I specialise in as a corporate coach is helping leaders understand who they are and aiding them to clearly understand the version of themselves that their colleagues, peers and subordinates see. I've always been an avid people-watcher and, as I mentioned previously, my skills of being able to read people and situations were honed as a young child at a basic level in order to survive, as I needed then to know how to gauge the temperature between my mum and dad and to make decisions as to whether preventative measures were required.

So when I started being trained in psychology and psychometric tools in order to do my particular job in HR, I began to see how some behaviour could be linked back to people's beliefs about what was expected. What is fascinating is that behaviour is documented all the way back to Hippocrates of Kos, the ancient Greek physician. Hippocrates identified four humours or temperaments he observed in people that he could base his medical diagnosis on.

In the context of corporate life, I'm sure that you may have been assessed at an interview using a tool that was designed to show how you would fit into the existing team, would make decisions and so on. I have heard many people shy away from attending assessment centres because they worry about being 'found out'.

What I did not understand so clearly before studying this topic was that if we spend our energy not being genuine, we can create in others and ourselves a lot of pain and confusion in trying to guess what people want to see. Now when I meet clients I make sure that we get to the bottom of who they really are.

We now live in an age where people who are in the public eye make a career out of being captured being 'themselves' in fly-on-the-wall documentaries or in other reality shows where they become celebrities. How many times have you heard, "Oh, they have got so big headed," or "Fame has really changed them," or even, "Who do they think they are?" after they have been part of such a programme. Some people behave in a way that they think is appropriate to go with the image they have. The sad thing for some of these people is that the persona or the behaviour they exhibit can be a long way from the real version of them, just like it was for my clients.

After a while, just as Emma found, wearing the mask 24/7 becomes draining and sometimes even celebrities forget which version of themselves should be on show – they can find themselves in hot water without really thinking about it.

But what if the issue isn't about our own behaviour but about someone else's? Emma adapted her behaviour because of her husband's style and it was only when she left that relationship that she could become the genuine version of herself. Many clients talk to me about managing their relationships with difficult colleagues and the effect that that situation has on how they show up.

One of my clients – Sarah, needed help in dealing with a difficult director where she worked. The situation that Sarah described was difficult in part because the director she struggled to work with had quite a brusque way of speaking to people, would use challenging behaviour in meetings and was reluctant to see the points of view of others. To me this style of leadership was pretty normal but when I asked Sarah to provide a physical description of the man in question I understood what was going on. Sarah was about 5ft 8'' and liked to wear shoes with a two to three inch heel; the director was about 5ft 6''. At some point in the past Sarah had heard the phrase 'little man syndrome' and because of her thinking associated with that, she had created a feeling and in turn behaviours that only saw negative interactions when dealing with this person.

My challenge was to get her to see what it was about her behaviour that may have been creating the difficulties. I made Sarah understand that when you have a problem you can only do one of three things:

- live with it

- fix it

- leave it.

This pattern of behaviour is also very prevalent in most other difficult relationships.

EXERCISE

Current problem

Think about a problem you have right now and write it down in one short sentence.

....

....

....

How does this problem make you feel?

....

....

....

How does this problem make you behave?

....

....

....

What is it about your behaviour that could be creating the problem?

....

....

....

If you can only choose one of the following in relation to your problem as a way to deal with it then which would you select and why?

- live with it

- fix it

- leave it.

Write down in as much detail the decision have you just made.

....

....

....

Now take appropriate action.

Sarah thought about the people that she was currently having 'difficult' relationships with. She recognised that her particular thoughts about the people were creating particular feelings that were, in turn, creating specific types of behaviour towards them. After exploring her behaviours with other colleagues and the reactions that those behaviours realised, she was willing to concede that some of the situations were in fact of her own making.

Having that clarity about your contribution to creating the environment where a difficult relationship exists is fundamental if you are to create opportunities to improve things.

With any client I ask them to think about other people they know who get on better with the individual they are having an issue with and see if they can identify what is different about the way they behave and what could be learned or copied in order to improve the relationship.

Sometimes this takes some probing but there will always be elements of the interaction that are different – don't discount anything.

I remember Guy who was a manager in a FTSE organisation who really struggled with this exercise. He didn't like his boss; he thought that he was 'an idiot'. However, he recognised that he needed to change his behaviour as his current mode of operating with his boss was career limiting. We explored how colleagues behaved with the boss and the only thing he could remember that was different about the interactions was that one colleague always knew how the boss's football team was doing. What Guy found frustrating was that this colleague also openly expressed distain about the boss – yet he apparently played a game to keep on the boss's right side.

As shallow as that piece of information may appear it was enough to make the boss relate differently to the colleague and was sufficient to mean that the colleague had a very different experience working for him.

Therefore, look at people who are having positive interactions with the person you are struggling to relate to and notice what they are doing that is different to you and then emulate them.

Sarah, who struggled to deal with her shorter director, decided to 'fix' things with him, so we discussed people who got on well with him and identified specifically what they did differently in the way they spoke to him or behaved around him and decided what she could try differently. The biggest light bulb moment for Sarah was when she was willing to explore, "What if she was 100% wrong?" about the director and the possibility that perhaps his behaviour was driven by the disdain that she clearly showed him.

Over a period of weeks Sarah noticed that the relationship was positively changing and, therefore, she felt and behaved differently, too. Within a few months things had improved significantly; the director was taking her into his confidence and asking her advice on sensitive issues. Over the couple of years that they worked together I know that Sarah grew to respect and value the director's opinion and guidance greatly and realised that had she not been willing to change her patterns of thinking then she would have missed this great opportunity.

From the bank of tests I've sat over the years I know how I show up and I am conscious of being as open, honest and genuine as I can be. However, it can be difficult if this isn't your area of expertise.

For example, I know that I'm driven and that I will do what it takes to get the job done *but* how I do this and the ways that I treat people in order to achieve my goals matters to me. From time to time I've had to work with people who appear more driven than me *but* because they place no value on the relationships of people around them they fail to see the effect that their behaviours have. When I'm working with some of my clients one of the things I may have to do for them is to help them understand how their style affects and influences the people around them and how they feel about other people's challenging styles in order to allow them to progress to the next level.

A couple of years ago one of my clients – Tom – was part of a Mastermind group of successful consultants. As a group they would get together on a monthly basis and support one another in growing their businesses. Part of the meeting was for people who wanted to share success, which Tom said he was always happy to do. Another part was to ask for help if anyone felt challenged. I have been part of similar groups and it is always inspiring to be with like-minded people and to share in others' success and to have the opportunity to be in the 'hot seat' and to get the benefit of others' wisdom.

When I checked with Tom whether he ever put himself in the 'hot seat' and asked his fellow consultants for help or support, he realised that he had not. In fact, on further probing, it dawned on him that he was only willing to share the good stuff and as such had created a persona in the group as a role model. Yet the truth was that Tom's business was struggling and he could have benefited massively from getting some other views and support from his peers. Some of the other Mastermind members had even told him that they wished they had his confidence and ability so he had decided that he didn't want to shatter their illusions. The respect of the people in that group mattered so much.

Then, unexpectedly, Tom was asked at a conference in London to share his story of how he had made the big changes in life that led him to be earning six figures. He felt elated at being noticed and for being asked and then he felt sick at the reality of standing up on stage and exposing himself for the fraud he then believed himself to be.

Tom had always been a take-action (eventually) person– but like Becca who created the challenge of experiencing '40 new things' in a year showed, if you put your mind to something you can make anything happen.

Tom accepted the speaking challenge even though letting people into his life was not something that he was either comfortable with or practised at doing and he admitted feeling afraid that he would suffer some form of rejection as a consequence.

As the moment approached to step up on to the stage in front of a room of 300 or so people, who had paid hundreds of pounds for their tickets, he described the feeling as being genuinely 'nervousandexcited.com'. His mouth went dry and as he looked out at the sea of expectant faces he realised that what they needed to hear wasn't the edited, glossy version of being successful but the warts-and-all version of how he had got to be the person they saw on stage and that actually what you see isn't always what you expect.

In that moment Tom truly stepped up to being the honest version of himself, he stopped being stuck and became EMPOWERED! He allowed himself to be vulnerable and exposed. He was willing to be rejected, ridiculed and derided. He remembers getting choked up talking about some of the very personal experiences he had had and was surprised by the amazingly positive reaction he received when he finished talking half an hour later. First, he got a standing ovation. Second, the number of people who wanted afterwards to shake his hand and spend time with him was a little bit overwhelming. Third, he received so many offers of help and support within a few short hours that he had enough work to put his business back on track.

In listening to the feedback Tom realised that he didn't appreciate what people who knew him saw him for and that actually in order to truly understand who he was, he just needed to ask people who was it that they saw.

EXERCISE

Showing up

In order to understand how you appear, try to understand how people see you. Here is a quick exercise that you can do in this vein with the help of your friends, family members and colleagues. If you split the responses into three different groups then it will allow you to see that there are variations of you that you perhaps hadn't realised existed.

Text or email as many people as you know and trust and ask them to send you a reply with the three words that they would use to describe you to someone else.

When you have collected all of the replies, type them exactly into a Word document, putting a comma between each new word. Retype (that is, do not exclude) any reoccurring words as often as you receive them.

Copy and paste the words from your Word document into a tool called www.Wordle.net

This will create an image for you. The words that appear in the largest and boldest font are the ones that appear most often in the responses you were given and are a strong indicator of the strengths or opportunities that are seen by the people who know you.

Here are the results for my own Wordle when I did this exercise. It was great to know how my clients and colleagues saw me.

SUMMARY

Presenting the most genuine version of you is vital to being able to live a happy and successful life.

Anything that deviates from that will take from you more energy and brainpower than it should. Be open to the fact that your thinking about a person or a situation may be 100% wrong and it would be good if you were willing to consider what could be different for you about them or it.

Trust that by sharing who you really are it will allow you to make better decisions about people, places and opportunities that are, or could be, available to you. If you realise that you have perhaps been presenting yourself to satisfy someone else's truth about who you are, get as clear as you can as to who you think you are when you are at your best and your happiest and then put your energies into making that version your default setting.

Chapter 5

PERSONAL BRAND

WITH

A GLASS OF FRESH ORANGE JUICE WITH A MARSHMALLOW DREAM BAR

Did you realise that you have a personal brand? I must confess that I never did until I trained as an image consultant – if I had realised it then I would not have made some of the hideous errors in colour, clothes and styling that I did, especially during my teenage years when I could have done with feeling extra-confident.

I did not give any thought to the image or message I was sending out into the world through the clothes and style I had created. Just like our personality gives an insight to those around us of our thinking, beliefs and values our clothes and body language can give indications of who we are and how we are feeling about ourselves.

Imagine that you have stepped on to a train and that you can see only two free seats. You have a four-hour journey ahead of you, so standing for that amount of time is not desirable. You take a moment to look at the passengers seated next to the empty seats.

The first option is to sit next to a smartly dressed, well-groomed but overweight male aged about 55. You notice that he has a small coffee stain on his shirt and he has a pile of documents – presumably work – on the table in front of him.

The second option is to sit next to a slightly dishevelled, slim, woman, who seems to be aged about 35. Her overall appearance is a bit grubby. She is tucking into a chocolate muffin and has on her table a hot drink.

So whom would you choose to sit next to?

People make judgments on what they see every day without even realising it. In the train seat exercise there is clearly no right or wrong answer and you may have even decided to stand until more seats became available but I guarantee your decision will have been influenced by the images that you saw.

If you look at five or six strangers on your way to work you could play a game and make assumptions as to their levels of education, how successful they are, whether they are married and the types of holidays they may take, just from looking at their clothes, accessories and the ways in which they carry themselves.

Just as I can help my clients understand themselves in terms of their motivation by using a personality test with them from my training as a behaviourist, I can also help them understand the message they give out by the choices they make when they are getting dressed in the morning because I trained as an image consultant.

For example, I know that the colour of the clothes I choose to wear on a daily basis affect my energy levels in getting things done, how confident I will feel with another person or in partaking in an activity and my decisiveness when I need to make important decisions.

I know that certain styles of clothes or outfits give me a confidence boost. This means that when I have had days that I knew were going to be difficult I would choose my clothes very carefully. If I needed to show up 'being in charge' then I would wear a tailored suit, usually black or navy, with a white tailored shirt underneath. If I needed to appear more approachable or sympathetic then I would wear something softer like a dress in pastel tones. Subliminally I was sending out a message from the minute that I was seen even before I opened my mouth.

Then I ensured my body language, voice, tone and words matched my intention so that all the information and messages I was giving out to whoever I was meeting or working with all lined up and was accepted as being authentic.

But imagine if I showed up in the same clothes but wanted to achieve the opposite impression. Would my sharp suit have created an approachable image? Would my pastel dress have said that I was in charge?

I remember seeing a communication model many years ago presented by a psychologist called Albert Mehrabian who believed that we communicate in three ways:

Body language and clothes: 55%

Tone and pitch of our voice: 38%

Words: 7%

I've used this model for myself and for lots of my clients with incredible results. I have helped them to understand the colours and style of clothes that not only suit their body shape but that are in line with their 'wardrobe personality' as well as working with them to understand their physical personality.

Understanding how to create the strongest personal brand for yourself that is right for where you want to be can positively affect your career, your relationships, your confidence and your perceived potential.

One of my friends gave me a tough bit of feedback once in my early career: "You should always dress for your next job, but my friend you don't even dress for your last one." I was stung, but she was right. I wanted to believe that I got judged on what I did not on how I looked. I did not see the link that people may make decisions on whether to speak to me, befriend me, promote me, give me additional responsibilities or ask me out based on how I looked.

Clothes are like armour or camouflage. We can use how we dress to protect ourselves, to show that we don't care or to show that we don't want to conform. We can even use how we dress to send out messages to say, "Help me!" or, "I'm OK."

Over the years I have worked with people who have suffered with severe depression and could spot their likely mood when they walked into the meeting just by noticing how they were dressed and the colours they had opted for.

Our image is a fascinating insight into our personal self-esteem. When I was a little girl my mum suffered for five years with undiagnosed depression. It went undiagnosed because she very carefully orchestrated a view to the outside world of a happy family. Inside it was a lot different and was probably where my interest in human motivation first was ignited.

I started to notice patterns with my mum around her appearance that allowed me to genuinely interpret how she was feeling. If she was having a 'good' day then she would wear bright colours and tailored styles that suited her body shape, would apply make-up and would style her hair. On 'bad' days she would wear one of two baggy, shapeless, dark outfits – the colours draining her skin tone, would probably not wear make-up (making her look ghostly) and I doubt she did more than run her fingers through her hair. Her appearance suggested that she was trying to make herself 'disappear'.

I remember that she would always be extra-'shouty' and emotional when she was in these clothes and, as a result, I was hyper-vigilant when I saw her in her 'bad day clothes'. Eventually, she did get the right help and support and the good day/bad day cycle got broken. We talked at length about whether she was aware of the difference in the clothes and colours she went for and, interestingly, she commented that on the days that she felt bad and had no energy it was almost like she could not see the nice, brighter, clothes in her wardrobe and she almost automatically grabbed the drab, shapeless things. Psychiatrists tell me that this is a very normal reaction when people are suffering from low moods.

A senior manager client of mine, who we will call Karen, came for support towards the end of her maternity leave. She had been suffering from postnatal depression but it had only just been diagnosed when I met her and she was due to return to work within a month and needed some help with her image and personal confidence. She had gone from being a high-flying career person with 95% control of her life to being a new, first-time mum who was struggling to adjust to the responsibilities of a baby. Her image crisis started when the baby was three weeks old. Karen had gone to the hairdressers for what she hoped would be a radical makeover in order to reclaim that she was someone in her own right other than being just a mum and had gone from having brown shoulder length hair to a peroxide blonde pixie close cut. This dramatic change in her physical appearance prompted her health visitor to explore how she was really feeling about being a mum and eventually, after a number of months, Karen admitted that truthfully she was struggling.

When we first started working together I asked if there were any specific occasions when she had been unhappy with her image. Karen related that through her pregnancy she had been unfortunate to suffer with severe sickness, which meant that she had actually worked from home a lot during this time and thus had become very comfortable in a casual style (as she did not need to dress smartly for work), which had continued after the baby was born. The trigger for the image crisis had occurred when she had received a wedding invite from one of her oldest friends who she hadn't seen for a while.

The dress code requested on the invite was black tie/ evening dress and as Karen was still at the stage of losing her baby weight she decided to hire something rather than buy an outfit that she thought she would probably not wear again. It was so painful listening to her recount this as she spoke of it in between loud, deep sobs.

Karen described the day in explicit detail. It was raining, dull and about 12 degrees. Because of her insecurity about her appearance and her lack of confidence doing something that was about being an adult again, she had chosen a dress to make her as invisible as possible – something dark and shapeless.

When I asked if she had tried on other things, Karen confirmed that she had but said that she had felt that nothing had looked right and the dress she had finally settled on – a long, aubergine, velvet dress as it – had felt nicest against her skin. The sad thing was that had Karen selected the dress before radically changing her hair it would have looked a lot better – but because she had changed her hair colour to something that neither suited her eyes or her skin tone she was completely right nothing would have looked that great.

In order to create the best personal brand for yourself it is important to understand and define what impression you want to show the outside world. Sometimes people do this when they need to make big changes in their lives. A friend of mine, Amy, needed to 'define her brand' when her marriage broke down and she unexpectedly found herself a single mum with two young daughters. Amy had left a large five-bedroomed family home and was renting a two-up two-down terraced cottage. There was not anywhere near enough space for all of her belongings. I remember helping her fill a skip with the stuff that she didn't need any more. She wanted to go through her clothes but knew that she was not disciplined enough to do it alone so she asked a couple of people she trusted most – including me – to go around one night and in effect make her over.

Amy's wardrobe was a mismatch of sizes, colours and styles. We were ruthless. She laughingly said that it was like watching locusts swarm as we went through the wardrobes and drawers sorting things into 'bin', 'charity' and 'keep'.

We filled five bin bags for the charity shop and filled one bag to be put out as rubbish, which only left a couple of pairs of pyjamas, a work suit, a casual dress, four tops and a pair of jeans for the 'keep' pile. However difficult it was, we all agreed that if we really wanted to help Amy, who we loved dearly, leaving her with stuff that didn't work for her was unfair.

In doing that exercise for Amy, I found an image consultant who analysed my own colours and bodyline so that I would not make costly mistakes for myself going forward. I have to say that it was a really enjoyable and fascinating process, and was one of the original reasons why I had trained as an image consultant.

Once I saw for myself which colours flattered my skin and hair tone I realised why so many of my old clothes had looked wrong. I could also see how knowing the right colours to wear would save me time and a massive amount of money when I went shopping for clothes.

The bodyline analysis was helpful as it explained to me why I had bought clothes in certain styles that never fitted properly and that therefore never looked as good as they should. By the end of the session I understood what I needed to have in a work wardrobe and in a casual wardrobe. I was also clear about the scale of accessories that would work better for me. I was delighted because straight away I dropped a skirt size just by buying the right cut for my body shape, so it did wonders for my confidence.

As an image consultant I have helped a lot of my clients understand the importance of wearing the right clothes to not only enhance how they feel about themselves but also how their friends and colleagues see them.

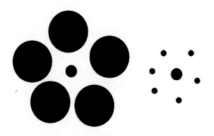

Have you ever seen diagrams similar to these?

Which middle circle is larger – the one on the left or the one on the right?

There will be some clever bods who knew that both of the middle circles were identical; what made them look different was the size of the circles around them. This is true of all patterns we wear on our clothes. The best scale for you will always be something close to your natural scale: small or petite = small scale; medium = medium scale; large = large scale.

The same applies to accessories – briefcases, handbags, jewellery and watches. If you wear or carry the wrong or an inappropriately scaled item then it will create a visual impression that is unflattering and inaccurate and may fail to draw attention to a part of your body that is your greatest asset.

To increase your confidence and the visual effect you make you have to understand your scale and your basic bodyline so that you can make the best choices from your wardrobe. Once you have this knowledge, even small changes can bring massive results.

Clients have asked for image assistance when they have had big or important events coming up. I have been able to show them how to dress appropriately for the situation using the rules that apply to their body shape. Where they have opted for items that don't flatter their shape or that are not the right colour, they will usually experience some mental or sometimes physical resistance that will hold them back from making the right impression.

A great example of this is dress-down days at work. If your usual working environment is fairly smart and you get a day to dress more casually, statistically it has been shown that you will be less productive that day and I would suggest a theory that it is linked to your brain associating what you wear to how much energy/brain power it needs to create for you. Likewise, people who have 'pyjama days' have reported that they get nothing done on those days.

One of my clients, who we will call Jeff, was a very senior executive but he didn't have a clue when it came to wearing clothes. Everything he had was either too large or too small and was badly cut for his build. He generally wore black suits and white shirts with a patterned coloured tie that drained his skin colour so that his colleagues were convinced that he was ill and was therefore not able to cope with the work they needed him to do. Jeff's hair hadn't been cut for a long time, although because of his age – he was 57, it wasn't growing that much. Sadly his personal grooming left something to be desired and I was told he often suffered with strong unpleasant body odour.

I was assigned the challenge of giving him the feedback on how he appeared to others so you can imagine that our first meeting was quite challenging and I had to ensure the clothes I wore gave me an image of well-groomed authority. Without clear insight Jeff was oblivious to his colleagues' views or the effect he was having on his colleagues.

Jeff was understandably embarrassed and hurt by my feedback but, to his credit, once he recovered from the shock of the honest and brutal conversation that we had, he was open to accept that if this was the reality other people saw, he had to do something to change it.

The great news was that with some coaching and education he was willing to have his colour and bodyline analysis done and the results were incredible. I admit that this was an extreme case, and a lot like many TV makeover shows, overnight his colleagues were able to see a change – just getting his hair cut and styled made a massive improvement.

They were bowled over by the change not just in his appearance but also in how he presented himself at work. Jeff confided in me months later that he felt happier and more confident than he could ever remember and he admitted that he kept looking at his reflection in mirrors and windows, each time being amazed that the reflection he saw was his own. The fact that his colleagues responded so warmly and positively to him boosted his confidence massively, especially as many of them asked him to share the secret of what he had learned so that they could mirror his reinvention.

How we present ourselves affects all of our relationships. Because I care about and respect everyone in my circle of friends and family, I always take a few seconds to notice what they are wearing and how they are behaving whenever I meet them because it is a good indicator of how they are feeling and I would hate to miss obvious indicators that they needed some help but didn't want to ask.

At work, our colleagues will make decisions about us based on how we dress and how we behave. At times this might be helpful or at times a massive hindrance.

In 2010 I surveyed the female Fortune 500 CEOs to find out what it was that made a difference to them in their careers and that helped them make it to the top jobs. All of those that responded mentioned the importance of creating the right impression with their bosses and their colleagues early on in their career.

Making an effort regarding how we look and how we behave should be for our benefit first rather than simply being about creating the right impression with friends, family members and colleagues. I know that when I make an effort with my appearance and my behaviour I feel more confident, have more energy and I am more successful. My friends and clients have reported the same correlation. It's almost as if we subliminally send a message to ourselves that we have confidence, belief and love for ourselves and people who present that way nearly always get the same feedback in a variety of guises from the people they interact with.

Personal Brand Quiz

Tick all of the answers that you believe apply to you.

General style

❏ Natural and comfortable   ❏ Not bothered about fashion ❏ Well coordinated and stylish ❏ Always appropriate ❏ Classic ❏ Creative ❏ Fashionable ❏ High maintenance ❏ Trendy ❏ Dramatic ❏ Expensive ❏ Designer ❏ Clashing styles

Choice of clothing: colour

❏ Bright ❏ Clashing ❏ Safe and conservative ❏ Colours that suit me ❏ Neutral (black, white, grey, brown) ❏ Soft pastel colours ❏ No idea which colours suit me ❏ Often wear patterned clothes

Choice of clothing: shape

❏ Tailored ❏ Well-fitting clothes ❏ Clothes that are too tight ❏ Clothes loose and baggy ❏ Figure hugging ❏ Clothes that flatter my body shape ❏ I don't know what really works for me

Personal grooming

❏ Overlooked ❏ Always wear make-up ❏ Do a full-length check before leaving the house every time ❏ Showering every morning ❏ Unshaven ❏ Never wear stained or worn clothes ❏ Well-fitted clothes ❏ Ironed clothes ❏ Hair always styled in the morning ❏ No dandruff

Body language

❏ Strong handshake ❏ Weak handshake ❏ Upright posture ❏ Slouched posture ❏ Comfortable posture ❏ Stiff posture ❏ Weight evenly distributed

❏ Weight mainly on one foot and hip ❏ Tendency to fold arms ❏ Tendency to put hands on hip ❏ Tendency to use hands to illustrate point ❏ Tendency to sit on hands ❏ Not sure what to do with arms ❏ Touches face frequently ❏ Hand over mouth ❏ Chews a pen ❏ Open and inviting hand gestures ❏ Often sit forwards ❏ Often sit back ❏ Often swing on a chair ❏ Crossed legs ❏ Sit with legs apart ❏ Sit with knees together

Facial expressions

❏ Often smiling ❏ Lots of eye contact ❏ Looking down frequently ❏ Frequently frowning ❏ Serious expression ❏ Deadpan

Movement

❏ Walks in a relaxed way ❏ Fast and purposeful when walking ❏ Strolls at a snail's pace ❏ Jerks knee or foot when sitting down ❏ Fidgets with keys/hair/face/mobile

Speech

❑ Soft ❑ Forceful ❑ Powerful ❑ Loud ❑ Distinctive ❑ Accented ❑ High-pitched ❑ Low-pitched ❑ Monotonous ❑ Using intonation ❑ Lacking in clarity ❑ Well paced ❑ Fast paced ❑ Slow paced

Use of language

❑ Use slang frequently ❑ Uses figurative language ❑ Swear frequently ❑ Brief, factual and to the point ❑ Frequently use hyperbole ❑ Often use humour, ❑ Don't finish sentences ❑ Use 'verbal mannerisms' too frequently (for example, a frequent use of 'umm' or a favourite phrase like 'sort of' or 'basically' or 'I mean') ❑ Use jargon ❑ Frequently agree with others ❑ Frequently disagree with others ❑ Never state own conclusions ❑ Always give opinions ❑ Always use language that is respectful of other people's race and religion

Behaviour

❑ Listen to and show an interest in others ❑ Dominate conversations ❑ Join in group activities ❑ Don't speak when in group situations, ❑ Encourage others to join in ❑ Interrupt others frequently ❑ Abrupt ❑ Remember people's names ❑ Direct about asking for what I want ❑ Take responsibility, ❑ Say 'no' firmly without causing offence ❑ Prone to emotional outbursts ❑ Emotionally sensitive ❑ Express feelings assertively ❑ Pay other people compliments ❑ Show sympathy for others ❑ Do not give up when faced with setbacks ❑ Strive for a job to be completed ❑ Frequently moody

Look over the boxes that you have ticked and ask yourself whether the factors that you have identified support the brand that you want to present. If you think that there is a gap between the image that you want to project and what you are currently doing then pick one or two areas you can work on that will contribute to you showing up in the way that will most represent the brand and impression you really want to give.

SUMMARY

Whether we realise it or not, we all have a personal brand. If we are confused about the messages that we want to convey and if we don't understand how to make the best out of natural attributes then we miss opportunities to communicate at a different level with everyone we come into contact with. Your reputation depends on you presenting yourself in the most effective and most appropriate way and if you do not care enough about how you appear, do not be surprised when you find yourself overlooked by others. They will take their lead in how they see you as treating yourself.

Talk with people you trust and ask them how they see you. Discuss with them how you would like to be seen and get ideas as to what you may need to change. If you can find an image consultant to work with then a colour and bodyline analysis is a brilliant investment. You will be able to save money as you will only be buying clothes that really work for you. You will save time, as you will very quickly see whether or not things in a shop work for you. Most importantly, you will feel fantastic.

Chapter 6

ROLE MODELS

WITH

A LARGE CAPPUCCINO WITH A FRUIT SCONE AND BUTTER

One of the ways that we learn strategies to deal with life, both the good and the bad, is by studying our role models. We may not realise that we are studying them but we absorb their thoughts and beliefs by just being around them.

My early female role models were my mum and my grandmother, both of whom I massively love and respect. My gran – from Cork in Ireland and one of 10 children – was an indomitable woman. Her family grew up around the railway industry and life was hard. There were no luxuries; it was all about keeping a roof over their heads, food on the table and clothes on their backs. My gran knew the value of working hard and despite having five children herself she managed to earn a living as a seamstress. Her work ethic definitely got passed down to my mum, who, in spite of later emotional difficulties, taught me that the only way to get what I wanted in life was through hard work.

My mum stopped work to raise my brother and I and then when I was in my 20s and married, my dad's business got into severe financial difficulties and even though she'd had a very long break she went and got a job working in in a care home. It must have been very difficult and even a bit humiliating to go and do something at that level, but she never complained: she was willing to do whatever she needed to do to help both the residents in the care home and my dad in keeping a roof over their heads. In fact, she only retired when she reached 70, which is an incredible achievement. I am immensely proud of her.

It cannot be a fluke that the work ethic of both of these women is part of my DNA. Just like my clients have shared with me in our sessions, there have been times when I have experienced things that have dented my confidence and depleted my energy and, in the very worst cases, made me want to take a duvet day. However, those feelings never last for long, as something kicks in that makes me 'keep going' and from somewhere deep inside. I'll find whatever it is I need in that moment to get back on track.

When I ask my clients about their role models they are often surprised, first, at who the significant ones are for them and, second, what the particular traits and attitudes are that they have knowingly and unknowingly adopted.

In lots of ways it does not matter who the role models were and whether they taught you good traits or bad traits as what matters is how you take these examples and use them to help you have the life that you want.

Occasionally, a client cannot immediately think of any good role models that they believe have influenced them but they can reel off a long list of negative role models. This is completely fine. There is a little known fact that you can be as successful as any of your heroes or heroines if you study them closely enough and then mimic everything they do – it will bring you results.

Another thing I have learned over time is that it is OK to not get everything right first time around; sometimes you will have to try something more than once. You need to have the opportunity at times to evaluate the results of your efforts enabling you to tweak or adapt your approach if you did not get exactly what you wanted as an outcome the first time.

Those that do well in life have an aura about them that is self-assured. They are people who understand the importance of relationships and who take the time to build rapport with the people who they have identified as sources of help or support to get where they want to be.

I describe people like this as 'always presenting themselves at 10 out of 10'. This means that they make the effort to show up in a very positive light; through their personal energy and optimism, the way that they speak and their body language they are natural magnets and people are drawn towards them.

Just think about a person you have really enjoyed spending time with. What was it that made the time enjoyable? Was it because they were miserable, grumpy or rude? Chances are *not*. It is more likely that they were entertaining, engaging and funny with a natural ability of making you and anyone else with them feel good.

So as a rule what type of person do you normally hang out with?

Who hangs out with you and why do you think they do that?

One of the ways to help you answer that is to think about who has been in your life so far.

The people we have around us will influence how we feel and how we compare ourselves in terms of assessing our relative success or failure.

When I get my clients to spend time thinking about the family and work colleagues who have left the greatest mark on them it can be quite a turning point in interpreting the things that they now do or believe. However, it also helps explain why they are the people that they are today.

One client – Liz – felt that her family were an interesting mix and described them to me like this:

> *Mum is such a wonderful woman; she is my rock and has taught me all the best qualities*

I recognise in myself. She is compassionate, caring and somehow knows instinctively what people need, especially if they are in pain or difficulty. In her 80 years of life she has been dealt some tough cards. Some she got over and some she found difficult to recover from. Because of those difficulties she has missed out on so much because she was not willing to move forward; she let her anger turn into hate, which meant overall I think she has had quite a sad life, weighted down by negativity. I really wish I could have helped her get over those things so she could have more happiness in her later years. Because of her experiences I promised myself if I ever suffered similar situations I would work to find a way to deal with the tough stuff so I did not miss out in the same way.

The great thing about this example is that Liz spotted a pattern of behaviour that she did not want to mimic because she recognised how it would hold her back.

Sometimes role models can be so hugely forceful in imprinting their beliefs and behaviour on us that it is difficult to see what is useful and what is not.

One entrepreneur, who we will call Simon, came for business coaching. On paper, he should have been earning seven figures but in reality he was struggling to even get to six figures. When we explored Simon's role models he talked about his father. Simon believed that his father was a good person overall but that his behaviour at different times was disappointing, making him feel confused about what he really should take from his dad. For example, Simon remembered being given support and encouragement to be his own person, especially when he first raised the idea of running his own business. However, if you engaged his dad on politics or other hot topics he could be arrogant, controversial and abrasive. As Simon's dad got older he cared less about what people thought of his wildly inflammatory comments, which invariably ended in argument and recriminations. Simon found this type of relationship draining and in later years he spent less and less time with his father. As a teenager, Simon had found out the hard way that his father had a different side, when he was about 14 his dad's business unexpectedly went into liquidation catching Simon and his mum completely by surprise. This was compounded weeks later when his dad walked out after 34 years of marriage.

Simon recognised that this experience taught him to avoid risk and to look for the safe options. He hated having heated debates with his dad or anyone else and therefore became a bit of a chameleon and appeared two-faced because he would agree with whatever was most popular in the moment rather than expressing his honest thoughts. He realised that he met and married his first long-term girlfriend at quite a young age just to create some stability after his home life imploded when his dad left and therefore it was no surprise that the relationship did not last more than five years as his wife realised that she did not know who her husband was. In understanding the effect that his father had had on him, Simon realised that he had purposely tried to create a pattern of behaviour completely different to what he believed his father displayed. With that clarity we were able to break the cycle of thinking/feeling and behaviour leading him to be at peace with who he really is.

Another client – Rachel, fondly spoke of her elder brother being a key role model. There was a seven-year age difference between them so she always felt a bit in awe of him and he was always very protective of her.

Her brother had red hair, pale skin and lots of freckles. Rachel was surprised to find out when she was much older that as a young child at school other children often bullied him because of his distinctive colouring.

Rachel remembered that when she was about three or four her brother got quite ill and was at home a lot with her and her mother. Fortunately, he made a full recovery, although Rachel reflected in one of our sessions that some of his illness may have been due to the bullying that he faced and it was his body's way of dealing with the stress. As an adult, Rachel's brother experienced the same sorts of knocks that we all do – broken heart, financial worries and fallouts with friends. He married at 30 and Rachel was chuffed to be asked to be a bridesmaid. After only two years of marriage his wife left him unexpectedly. While he didn't let the bitterness show very often, Rachel noticed that within a year of that setback he had dropped his expectations for himself massively. He had been an average student but was great with people and seemed well thought of by his bosses. Rachel was struggling with this switch in his outlook because she held him up as a massive role model for herself and because he was shaken, she in turn then doubted her own ability to deal with similar setbacks.

Through our conversations I have enabled Rachel to realise that she is free to make her own choices in how she deals with any situation that affects her in the future. I have also got her to accept that while she loves her brother it has nothing to do with her what he decides he wants for himself and worrying about it is not serving her happiness at all.

Many clients come and it is their current or ex-partner that has been a significant role model in their lives. One client, Maria, remembers her ex pondering if they had ever truly loved each other as they were separating, which made her believe that she would never trust anyone else because she had loved him and had thought that he loved her.

Another client, who we will call Joy, felt resentful when her husband was unfaithful because of what she believed she had given him. Joy thought that he was misunderstood with hidden potential when she first met him and she had done everything to mould him into the person she thought he should be. Her light bulb moment was when I paraphrased back to her what I had heard her say and she realised that part of the reason he looked elsewhere was possibly because he did not feel good enough because she was always trying to 'change him'.

When we dug deeper at what the truth in that situation was, it was brought to the surface that Joy had grown up with a lot of negative messages from her father about her ability. She believed that if she could help someone achieve greater potential then that would make her successful through a halo effect. Joy had to learn that people have to want to access that potential for themselves and not be pushed against their will.

There are clients who have achieved measures of success and who find themselves dealing with a jealous or unsupportive partner. Sometimes they realise that they are following a pattern they observed in their own parents and that the reason they may have been attracted to the person in the first place was that the behaviour and ritual that went with the relationship felt familiar.

In the majority of these cases they had a belief that they would have a different ending to that of their parents and then became frustrated when they had the same, or in a couple of extreme cases, worse, outcomes.

When I was growing up, if we needed to travel anywhere – pre-satellite navigation systems – my dad always took total responsibility for getting us there: physically and planning out the journey. In fact my mum didn't learn to drive until she was in her late 30s. It therefore came as a big shock to me that when I went to new places in the car with my now ex-husband that he expected me to map-read for him. I hated map-reading, as I had a belief that I wasn't any good at it. We had gone on a journey that should have taken about three hours, but I had made several mistakes. I was becoming increasingly nervous and flustered.

Instead of being supportive and offering to help, my husband at the time slammed the brakes on, shouted some insults at me, snatched the map book out of my hand, opened his window and threw the book out of the window onto the grass verge. He then set off at speed with the wheels spinning. I recognised that his anger was as a result of my incompetence, so I just kept quiet. The funny thing was that in throwing the map out of the window he had thrown away the very thing that he needed to help us get home.

If we had ever had a conversation about how his parents had typically got from A to B, I would have learned that his mum was the person responsible for map-reading and his dad took no responsibility for getting the family to their destination. With that set-up as a role model it is unsurprising that my ex would expect me to fulfil the same role for him.

It took a while but in understanding who his role models were I began to understand him a lot more.

EXERCISE

Role models

Who are the people that you consider to be significant role models in your life?

....

....

....

....

What are the things you recognise they have taught you?

....

....

....

....

Are there particular patterns of behaviour you know you have that no longer serve you?

....

....

....

....

If there was one thing that you could change that would help you to move forward one or two steps what would it be?

....

....

....

....

When can you commit to making that change?

....

....

....

....

....

What is interesting to point out to you as I do to my clients is that just as we have been influenced we in turn become influencers. I have two gorgeous daughters and I am very conscious of the fact that I am a role model to them. There are times when I have to ask myself what it is that I am trying to teach or show my daughters about life in the way that I speak and behave.

I work with many clients who come to see me for support in their professional lives and as part of that process we will chat about things that are going on in their lives outside of the office.

They all have stories that are about challenges or difficulties they have experienced and while they may not have realised it before we started working together the thing they come to understand is that if they have a history that they wish they didn't then they don't have to let that history own them – they can change their future.

One client I worked with, who we will call Clare, grew up with a mother who suffered with severe depression and when she was about 16 Clare's father left the family home because he felt that he couldn't cope. As Clare grew into adulthood she married quite young and sadly also suffered spells of depression herself, which her own husband found very difficult to deal with. As a couple they went to marriage counselling to work through their difficulties. What Clare heard in one particular session was the counsellor accusing her of being a victim and suggesting that if she carried on following the same patterns of behaviour she would be creating a self-fulfilling prophecy in that her husband would leave her like her father left her mum.

I am sure the counsellor's intention, if Clare's recollection and interpretation was correct, was to shock Clare out of the pattern of behaviour she had heard described to her. Unfortunately, it didn't, and Clare decided to leave her husband before he had the chance to do it to her first. For a long time afterwards, she told me that she blamed the counsellor for the breakdown of her marriage as she had felt backed into a corner after that particular session and feared she would carry on living a life being depressed just like her mum.

In working together Clare focused on accepting the experiences for what they had given her – which was a list of things she would not choose in the same situation. She created some options for what she would choose instead.

I know when I stop and reflect on my own life and where I am right now that if I had not had the experiences and interactions that I did have then I would not be the person that I am today.

SUMMARY

Experiences we have had in the past do not need to be the basis on which we define our future. Every single person we have come into contact with – even those we do not now remember – will have left an impression on us. . The people who influence and shape us from our early years have a belief that their 'map of the world' is correct, regardless of how screwed up that may seem. Whatever you believe to be true for you about the experiences you have had, don't let them be the reason that you stay put in an unhappy life. Use the exercises to help you learn what you need and then come up with a plan of how you can do something different to move to another level.

Chapter 7

WORK EXPERIENCE

WITH

A LARGE ICED CAFFÈ MOCHA WITH A CINNAMON ROLL

Just as my family have left a mark on who I am, so have my friends and so have my work colleagues, and by the same token I must have had the same effect on people I've worked with, too.

For example, I definitely believe in enlightened mentorship and whenever I have had the opportunity to mentor someone, either formally or informally, I've tried to be there for them as a supporter, as a confidant or just as a sounding board. The reason that doing this matters to me is because I know that some of my success can be attributed to the fact that a number of key people in the businesses I have worked in saw my potential and found ways to help me make my leap and step up – even when I doubted it myself.

In my career I've had the pleasure and the misfortune of working with some fabulous and some despicable people and yet in reflecting on all of those experiences I know that I have learned from each and every person. One of my best bosses was a director called Alan, who ran a regional division of a global engineering company. When I started working for this company I was one of 22 women out of an office of 335 people. I worked in administration and in HR but I was really interested in understanding how the technical stuff that went on in the office got done. So I asked questions. Alan clearly thought that this showed good initiative on my part and he would share lots of information with me; Alan explained to me how bids for jobs were put together and would ask me questions regarding how I thought things could be improved. Because he shared his knowledge and encouraged me to do more in the office environment I found myself managing a team of people and being sent to university in the evening to get a business degree.

Another fabulous boss, Amanda, taught me that it was OK to not have all the answers and that it was good to use the wider team to solve problems and that it was important to create opportunities equally for everyone. During this phase of my career I was involved in some pretty major organisational restructuring yet because of her leadership style she empowered all of us to believe that we had responsibility for our piece of the project and that should we need her assistance she was there. That someone was willing to have that much trust in my ability was essential in order for me to step up to another level. As a result of that opportunity I was promoted again to a much bigger role and I was eventually headhunted out of that business to go into a role another two levels up, paying 40% more.

But where there is ying, there is yang. In my time I have worked for some real tyrants, too – both interestingly HR directors.

The male version was just a sexist bully, but he was clever; he knew how far across the line he could go so that it could still be open to interpretation. The female version identified what a person's weak spot was and then went for it time and again. Her behaviour was erratic so you never knew what was going on, passive then aggressive. It was a time in my life where I was definitely living on eggshells. Some of the rules in the office she reigned over included: mobile phones had to be on silent (apart from hers), laughter was frowned on, nothing hanging on chairs, no eating at desks – it went on. I remember being totally gobsmacked when she asked me a question one day that was on a part of the business I would have had no knowledge of and then when I looked blankly at her she said "Don't worry your pretty little head about it." If it had been an interaction in a private office that would have been bad enough, however this was said at volume in an open plan office. Weeks later colleagues were asking me, in jest, "how's your pretty little head today?" not realising I had felt humiliated.

So you see these experiences shape my perception of what traits and talents are required to be a good boss, which I hope my subordinates have benefited from.

As a boss myself I've had some fantastic people work for me over many years. Some have been very different and challenging personalities, some have been collaborative and similar in outlook to me. I know that I have a tendency to be a little bit lastminute.com, which for more planning orientated personalities will be a challenge. I have always asked anyone who has ever worked for me to define how he or she would like to be managed and then tried to honour the information they shared.

What I realised as I started to climb the career ladder is that the higher up you get the smaller your peer group and how the relationship is different at this level. For example at entry level or junior roles you hopefully will see everyone on the same level as you as a potential mate and ally. People ask for help, support and advice willingly at this level and statistically people at this stage of their career are more likely to socialise with each other assuming that where people work and live is compatible.

As the peer group gets smaller it is more likely that you will start to see each other as competition and therefore be a bit more wary of sharing too much. It is less likely you will ask for help and the number of people we naturally trust becomes a lot smaller. Socialising begins to be for work related reasons rather than out of choice.

Do you recognise any of this?

Some of my clients have left roles in order to climb the career ladder so they don't have the longevity and history with their new colleagues. They cite this as being a reason for having superficial relationships with work colleagues instead of the relationships some very successful men and women have who have worked in their organisations for 20+ years, climbed the ladder through recognition, and have had the support of the work force that know and trust them.

In fact another surprising fact that came out from doing my research with the female CEOs in the Fortune 500 companies was that I learned that more than half of them had worked for the same organisations for 20+ years. Also, what is interesting to note, is that in the intervening years the couple of ladies who had been brought into the top job as external hires have all been replaced by other long serving members of staff of the employing company.

A number of my female clients have shared a fear of not being able to cope if they put themselves forward for bigger roles and so they make a conscious decision not to do it. This is quite sad because when I ask them what is the real reason behind that belief it comes from having worked for female managers themselves and either seeing them sidestep opportunities or having had conversations where they collude "why would you want that extra responsibility" so there are few great role models to follow.

Be honest with yourself; what kind of colleague are you? If you had to get some 360-degree feedback from five or six people at work at different levels what might they say? Even if you think they don't know you there are a lot of things you can do to make better connections without the need to sell your soul. I have helped so many of my clients understand how they are seen and what they can do if they need to change that view that we have already covered in previous chapters.

Let's think about our friends – what do they bring to us? One of my mentors and coaches told me many years ago that if I was serious about being successful I needed to spend time with successful people. At first I laughed and said that was very shallow, but then I realised there was some truth in what they were saying. If I spent my time with people who weren't interested in putting the effort into growing their career and just moaned and groaned about their lives, it was draining, very draining and the relationships were very one way. However, by creating an environment and spending time with people who shared a similar interest and motivation, it was so much more energising and it allowed me to find new momentum to access my next level of potential.

So you see if you find your mood is going up and down just ask yourself who are you spending time with and what energy and support are you and they getting from spending time together.

I know that through all my life's up and downs there are some very special people who have stood by me through thick and thin. They have seen me at my lowest and yet they still love me, they have been there when things are going well and encouraged me. They regularly tell me they use my life as a barometer for how well they are doing and they love the fact that spending time with me reminds them they have things quite easy. I confess doing what I do as a coach and hearing some of my clients' stories is a great leveller for me too.

Whatever the truth is, I know that I am a much better person from having these people in my life. Someone once said to me that people come into our lives for a reason, a season or a lifetime and when I think about all the people I've known it is true.

I can think of many faces and names of people who flitted in and sit in 'the reason' category. Even friends met on holiday over my childhood years, those brief interactions ensured the one or two weeks were fun, happy and memorable. I had penfriends – in the days before computers and mobile phones where you had to wait days or weeks for interaction with friends. I had at least two girls I wrote to for many years but I never met either of them, yet through my early teens I would share information and even the odd secret or two. I'd even class a couple of flings after my marriage fell apart in this category. As I only really had one serious boyfriend before I got married, when that ended, I was curious to know whether other men would find me attractive.

Then, there are a group of people who appeared for 'a season' – work colleagues, school friends, mums at NCT classes, people I met on courses, the list is huge. At the time these people were in my life nine times out of ten they were adding to it in a positive way. Those that I see in the tiny one out of ten pile, knowing them may not always have been fun but they still taught me bits of useful stuff.

Finally, are the group who are in it for the long haul and it's OK that in times to come some of them may move into 'a season' category just because the things that keep us connected right now may no longer be there. This special and unique group love me unconditionally, forgive me when I mess up, support me when I feel vulnerable and generally know when I need space and when I need to be dragged out of my cave and into the land of laughter. They are my teachers, my role models and my mentors.

No matter where you are in your life, I want you to know that everything and everyone who makes up your story are there for the right reasons – even if it isn't clear what that is.

EXERCISE

Significant people

I'm sure as you have been reading this chapter that you have been mentally sorting out where you would put the people in your life. Well what I want you to do is jot their names down and really think about what their relationship means or has meant to you. Include everyone who has been of significance in your life even if it was for negative reasons. Just reframe what the learning was in a different context. For example, someone who may have been a bully or been abusive to you may have taught you what elements in a relationship you won't accept. Understanding what we don't want helps us get closer to what we do want.

A reason	A season	A lifetime

As I have already explained, both of the HR directors who were awful bullies taught me how *not* to treat people and I am a natural optimist and chose to believe that part of the reason why they have behaved in the ways that they did towards me was that they were a little bit envious of the way that I found it easy to build relationships and rapport with people, a skill neither of them had. Does the way that they treated me and the way that it made me feel still rankle on occasions? Hell yes. I wish I had been more courageous at the time and that I had stood up to them. However, that time has passed, and in order to find a way to be able to change the effect and the importance that I was attaching to it, I found that challenging myself to find a positive outcome was a much more empowering way to deal with it.

I know from my own experiences, and that of many of my clients, the only way to change the rubbish/blockers is to 'Just Do It' and that was how my company JDI Creative Solutions Ltd came to exist. JDI (Just Do It) was as much a message to myself as it was to anyone else.

Years ago I did an exercise with a coach where I had to think about what I would want the six year-old me to know if I was to travel back in time and have a meeting with myself at that age. I remember crying deep, sobbing tears during this activity (which came as a huge surprise), but it was a simple message that I felt would be of most use to her: 'Do not worry. No matter how hard or difficult the things are that may come along you will be OK.'

EXERCISE

Talking to the younger you

I want you to get into a place where you can just relax for a couple of minutes. You may find it helpful to close your eyes and take a few deep breaths. Imagine that you can now see a younger version of yourself at a time when you most needed support. Regardless of what was going on for you at that age, the image you can see is a time when you were safe and well. You now have the chance to have a conversation and impart something that will make a massive difference. What message did you need to hear?

Imagine yourself saying the words and imagine getting a response.

Give yourself a hug.

Clap your hands once.

Notice what feels different and if any of your thinking and beliefs about something has changed.

SUMMARY

For many of us being at work will form the biggest chunk of our lives. It is therefore vital to our wellbeing to recognise who is responsible in this area of our lives in order to create as positive an experience as possible.

The buck stops with *you*.

I talk regularly to clients who want help with career changes or dealing with colleagues and they are often caught off guard when I ask, "What is it about your behaviour that is creating that situation?"

If we are receiving behaviour that we don't like then we can alter our behaviour to see if we get a different response. We can also talk to the individuals involved and check if our understanding about a situation is correct. If you need to give someone some feedback or need to check something out then you can use a simple model:

Context (what happened and when)

+

Behaviour (what did you see or notice)

+

Effect (how did it make your feel)

+

Next steps (what do you want to see changed or repeated)

=

An honest adult conversation.

If you don't get the result that you want then remember the options: live with it, fix it or leave it.

Don't settle for something that makes you unhappy, You owe it to yourself and your wellbeing to role model the best behaviour for yourself rather than waiting for everyone else to take care of you.

Chapter 8

CHALLENGING BELIEF

WITH

A POT OF EARL GREY LAVENDER LOOSE LEAF BLACK TEA AND A SLICE OF FRUIT TOAST

Time and again I have worked with clients who have used where their point of origin was as a way of excusing why it is that they weren't more successful in love, life and/or finances. When I tell them that they are mistaken and that the only person with the ability to hold them back is actually themselves, they typically become defensive.

So why do I think that you have the power to rise above and go beyond wherever your parents or guardians started you off?

Since time began the way that we have had knowledge and learning imparted to us has been a bit like doing a huge jigsaw but without having a picture to follow. From our earliest moments we are with people who act as our elders, teachers and role models and we have already considered the effect they have on us. They fill our environment and our brain space with things that they were themselves taught or that they themselves experienced. Their intentions are normally well meant – at its basic form, their intentions are usually to protect and provide.

The only downside to this is that each bit of information we have been given has embedded in it the other person's interpretation or belief. For example, my ex-husband doesn't like tomatoes. His mum doesn't like tomatoes. Even though I keep trying, my two daughters refuse to eat tomatoes.

The same psychology applies to reactions to animals. I know people who are afraid of a certain type of animal and when I've asked what the particular experience was that gave them that fear in the majority of the cases they do not report a bad personal experience but talk instead of having inherited the fear from someone very close to them who didn't like that particular animal.

Without realising it, the myths, legends and beliefs of our tribe get passed down and embedded into us on such a subconscious level that we frequently don't question or even have any particular awareness of it happening.

Geography is another topic that comes up when I'm challenging my clients on achieving their potential. I did some career coaching with some young people in Wolverhampton a few years ago. The city had mass unemployment and needed considerable investment and regeneration. One conversation that rocked me to the core was their belief that it would bring shame to their families if they got off benefit and got paid work simply because in five or six generations of the same family no one had ever had a job. Out of the many thousands of career conversations I've had over the years this one sticks in my mind the most because of the sense of hopelessness behind the intention.

My challenge was to open up their minds to the possibility of what having paid employment may mean for them as individuals and for their families in the future. Yet this group was not unique; they are part of a large statistic that the government tries to find new and different ways to manage. In most western countries there will be families who, for whatever reason, find themselves supported by the state and after a while it almost becomes easier to let yourself believe that that is your potential and to stop doing anything about it. Problems then arise when the state changes the goal posts and requires new behaviour that individuals feel that they unable to cope with.

As I've already explained, a lot of the information that we pick up from key people who influence us is on a subconscious level. We may not even know what it is that we know about them. It is interesting that we let some of this stuff form the boundaries to the goals we set ourselves. Living life without a goal or a direction is like trying to knit jam – it just is not going to happen. I've always had little goals, but when I've thought about it they always had a materialistic edge: Earn more; Have more; Be more. I would set myself up to fail quite regularly and then, metaphorically, beat myself up – for being weak, sad and pathetic – when I failed. I also know that I'm not alone in this. Every single person, at some point, doubts himself or herself and/or measures himself or herself against someone who is seemingly doing better than they are.

One of my mentors, Richard Wilkins, who is the master at the Ministry of Inspiration, has said that the only goal any one of us should have is simple: To not be dead.

Richard came to this startling realisation after working in a hospice for six months after a friend of his was admitted. He noticed that instead of being a place of gloom and doom there was much energy, possibly because the patients were more awake to life than the people outside that environment. Many had let go of the stuff that really did not matter.

One of the things I learned from Richard is that, unwittingly, I had the power to control all of the negative thinking that was happening to me.

A lot of the things that I used to think about myself came from how I interpreted the behaviour of the key people in my life. It wasn't until I tried to put myself in their shoes and imagined what the world looked like from their point of view that my thinking changed.

I used the same techniques with my clients. Lara (see chapter 1) realised that her father probably felt a bit shut out after he and her mum had children and then with her granddad dying so soon after her brother was born he would have felt even more of an outsider as he wasn't the person who needed the most help. Her mum clearly withdrew from him to give her energy to her grieving mum, to Lara and to Lara's young brother. Lara realised that this probably resulted in her dad feeling rejected and thus he had started to look for comfort in other places.

When Emma (chapter 4) thought about her ex-husband she realised that he may have been hugely jealous of and a bit intimidated by her bubbly personality and her ability to make friends and find opportunities so easily where he had a more awkward approach in social situations. By undermining her confidence and by being sarcastic and scathing about her abilities Emma realised that he was trying to create in her a dependency on him for her needs. This technique had worked up to a point, particularly as Emma was brought up Catholic and believed that marriage should be forever and thus tried her best to find ways to survive in that environment. Interestingly, it was only when Emma had the children that she found the courage to break out, as she did not want their upbringing to have the same highs and lows that she had experienced.

Waking clients up to the damage their thinking, their feelings and their behaviour is having on limiting their potential is hugely rewarding. It takes time to realise that these three elements can be the cause of sabotaging and stagnating the ability to be empowered.

For example, Emma now chooses to believe that (and in turn feel and act as if) her ex-husband wants her to do well and provide their daughters with great opportunities and be a strong and steady role model for them.

Clare (see chapter 6) reframed her view of her father and why it was that he left the family home. She chose to believe that he didn't know how sad and lonely her mum was because she knew that her mum was very stoic and whenever asked, "Is everything ok?" she would always respond in the affirmative with a beaming smile. Therefore, she accepts that her dad's intention in leaving was to do with keeping himself sane.

One of my goals is to be a good mum. Being a parent brings huge responsibilities that no one can ever really prepare you for. Setting aside the practical support that a baby needs, there is no denying that at the start it is difficult, tiring and an emotional rollercoaster. The idea that as they grow and become more independent it equates with an easier life is a complete myth. In fact, it actually becomes much tougher, simply because everything you do and everything you say is your way of imparting a tiny bit of your jigsaw puzzle to your children or your charges and as independent thinkers they will question, challenge and disagree just like you did. Of course, there are many joyful, happy aspects to being a parent but because so few of us live in the present we are usually distracted and miss them.

I continually ask myself what it is that I want to give my girls. I know that because of my upbringing and my experiences I am probably too independent and self-reliant. I often find it difficult to ask for help or assistance with things. Being a coach I am used to people seeking me out for help and support but personally I have been wary about letting people into my world.

Trust matters a lot to me and to most of my clients, probably because we can recall times that we have been let down (badly) by people whom we felt we should have been able to rely on. However, because I understand their profiles, and mine, I am able to explain or open them up to the possibility that rejection is just something that they fear and that they should pay attention to the feeling that is created by that belief. Changing the belief is the gateway to something wonderful.

SUMMARY

Accepting that we are all a work-in-progress is usually a massive relief to the clients that I work with.

It is completely OK if they haven't put themselves forward for promotion or purchased a property or taken up a course or gone out on a date with someone. There could be very good reasons that the time wasn't right for that stuff to happen or to come into their lives.

Beating yourself up about something is not going to change the situation.

The more we can work on letting go and changing our view of the stuff in our past that is holding us back the easier it is to start seeing options that may have been hidden before.

Swapping a couple of words in the language we use with ourselves can make a massive difference, too. Use 'will' instead of 'should'. Use 'how can' instead of 'can't'. Use 'I feel' instead of 'I think'.

I worked with a wonderful lady a while ago who showed me the difference that could be achieved just by saying out loud to ourselves, "I'm OK." Because our ears hear it, our brain thinks it and our physiology changes.

You are already amazing just as you are, so start telling yourself that and believe that it is true and notice when great things start happening.

Chapter 9

MOVING THE MOUNTAIN

WITH

A LARGE HOT CHOCOLATE WITH WHIPPED CREAM AND MARSHMALLOWS

Sometimes clients I've worked with just weren't ready to be honest with themselves about what they really needed to work on when they came with a problem. They seemed reluctant about being specific as to what the issue was that was holding them back, or confused as to what exactly the issue was.

I would hear, "I don't know" or, "I'm not sure" a lot.

If their company was paying for them to have the conversation with me, then they sometimes presented themselves as if they were just going through the motions to tick a box that appeared on their appraisal.

I would suggest that as we were going to spend time together anyway, I was happy to help them with any aspect of their lives and as our sessions were confidential the people at their workplace would never know. I have never had a session with a client when there wasn't something that they needed to work on.

Everyone will get to a crossroads in their life when they decide that they want something different or that they need to make a change. Sometimes this feeling can be triggered by a big event, be it one that you are personally caught up in or something on a much bigger scale. For example, I remember being six months pregnant when I saw on television the twin towers of the World Trade Center in New York come down on 11 September 2001 and feeling a sense of panic about the type of world I was bringing new life into.

If and when you get to that crossroads, the thing that will help you is to stay calm and to be open to exploring what you *can* do rather than focusing on what is outside of your control. Panicking or getting paralysed will not help you – no matter how scary you believe the situation to be.

All of the courses and training I have done have been for the purposes of finding the secret in being happy and filling a hole and making me feel better, partly because I thought I was incomplete and that something was missing. I wanted to be happy – genuinely, Earth-shatteringly, happy. Yet despite everything I had I could not see that my thinking was stopping me see that I already had everything at my fingertips to make me that happy.

I now know that I am *enough*, just as you are – and that while there will still be things you and I will want to achieve through our lives we need to be aware that the only person putting us under the pressure that makes us feel overwhelmed, disempowered or stuck will be ourselves.

One of the things I work to get my clients to realise is that they have never failed at anything they have tried. I get them to look at situations or experiences where they did not get the results that they expected or wanted and get them to consider these situations as if they were merely undertaking research and that the results or outcomes didn't really matter as they were just trying to work out what worked for them and what did not.

If every scientist gave up the first time an experiment failed then we would not have the medicines to fight killer diseases that we have now.

Do you have a hole that you are trying to fill or a sense that something is missing for you? Do you have a belief where the hole is?

EXERCISE

Happy test

This exercise is quick and easy and is designed to help you think about where in your life you are happy and where you have scope for more happiness.

Give yourself a score from 1 to 10 against each of the following categories of how happy you are with each aspect in your life.

1= miserable

10 = ecstatic

Personal development:

Purpose/Career/Job:

Finance:

Health:

Body:

Intimate relationship:

Family:

Physical fitness:

Mental/Emotional:

Social:

Now add up the answers against each area and that is the % you are happy with your life.

...% happy with life

The bulk of the population will score from 50% to 60% on average so anything more than that and you are doing well.

When you think about each element that you did not give a score of 10 to, what do you believe needs to happen in order to move it from whatever number you gave it to 10?

I want you to start thinking about creating a map that will help you become clear on what the things are that you want out of life.

As I have already explained previously, one of the things that disempowers us and creates the sense of feeling stuck is that we begin comparing ourselves to other people we know and, as I'm sure you will have noticed, we aren't generally that kind to ourselves.

So before we start to come up with some goals to work towards in order to be happier, the first question I want you to think about is whether when you scored yourself on this test you were comparing yourself to anyone/several other people and could that have affected the score that you gave yourself.

Lots of my clients find it difficult to reframe their negative thinking when they first start working with me, but this is only a pattern of behaviour and, with practise, they soon get the hang of it. And if they ever slip back every now and again into the negative thinking, it does not matter as long as they notice what they are doing and decide if that approach is working for them in that moment and if it isn't then they realise that they do have a set of behaviours they can use instead.

Negative thinking usually has a 'can't' or a 'not' in it somewhere. These statements are not empowering, inspiring or dynamic in any way, but they are incredibly powerful in placing an invisible force field around us that keeps us stuck.

What we need to do is create the antidote to this force field. I usually ask my clients to come up with some enabling statements that mean something to them about the areas they want to focus on.

For example, Emma (see chapter 4) believed that she had done the wrong thing breaking up with her husband even though she was desperately unhappy; her initial statement was: "I am not a good mum because I broke the family up." This statement was very disempowering and encouraged Emma to have negative feelings about herself and affected how she parented her children. She developed a behaviour of overcompensating because of what she believed and as a result found it a challenge on occasions to say "no" when being pushed for something, especially by her youngest child.

However, when she reframed the statement it became, "Because I am a good mum, I wanted my children to grow up in a happy and stable environment. I could only do that by living apart from their dad."

This states clearly what her positive intention was about bringing the marriage to an end and in shifting her mindset meant that she felt empowered to be a strong and resolute parent who had no need to apologise or make things right.

When Tom (see chapter 4) came to see me, his statement of what he believed to be true about himself was, "I can't tell people my business is in trouble because they will lose respect for me and see me as the fraud that I am."

He admitted this statement would play round and round in his head in various forms whenever he thought about talking to someone and asking for help – so he was really paralysed – and recognised after talking about the situation that nothing would have changed if he stayed in the place he was in.

When he thought about a more empowering statement for himself he came up with, "When I talk openly and honestly about the challenges I face being in business, I allow people the chance to swap advice with me, which has the power to help all of us."

Becca's experiences meant that she feared rejection and her behaviour stopped her from taking chances in her career and in life. Her statement was probably one of the harshest I have heard "I don't trust people to do the right thing by me so it is easier to expect to be disappointed and that way I will never be hurt."

What was difficult for Becca (see chapter 3) to understand and accept was that in holding that belief about herself she had put on a pair of blinkers so that when positive opportunities presented themselves she couldn't see them. She realised that the type of men she had dated were generally quiet and unambitious types who bored her quickly. We also explored if there were people in her life she trusted and of course she came up with the names of friends, family members and some colleagues, which surprised her. The more empowered statement had a completely different feel. "I recognise I have lots of great people in my life and I believe there are exciting opportunities and experiences waiting for me. I trust myself to make great decisions about which ones to take and know my friends and family will support me."

The key bit about Becca's statement for me was, "I trust myself." When she first started working with me Becca did not understand the concept of conducting research and that where she had done things in the past that hadn't worked it was not failure on her part but rather her way of finding out what would work for her and what wouldn't. Once I got her to accept that there was no failure she realised that the issue wasn't about anyone else: It was that she didn't trust herself to make good choices.

Could that be you, too?

I've worked with occupational psychologists, psychiatrists, counsellors and other mental health experts over the last 20 years and they continually tell me that one of the biggest things people don't do is hold positive images of themselves. Even really successful people will tell you what their flaws are, rather than what the things are that they do well. In just the last five or so years I've seen a flurry of activity in the coaching provider space where there has been an explosion in coaching that helps people become more confident.

I know that there were definite events in my past that I recognise as being transformational and not necessarily for good reasons. However, just as I have found and taught my clients the challenges, the unfulfilled dreams, the disappointments and worse don't have to be the reason to give up and settle and if we break them down into bite-size chunks then they won't be the things that keep us stuck any more.

When I look at my daughters I know that, just as my parents taught me (whether intentionally or not) how to think, feel and believe about life, I am doing the same for them and I want to do my best to show them that anything is possible. I also let them teach me to be more open to possibilities that they don't even know exist yet and that they can choose.

Have you ever noticed how children use their imagination to fill in the gaps of their knowledge? They may not know how spaceships get to the moon but that does not stop them when they are playing. They have such a magical way of creating ideas and opportunities because they haven't learned to listen to their inner voice telling them that something they are doing is silly, stupid, irresponsible or childish. Some of the most amazing inventions of the modern age came from someone having an idea and ignoring the hundreds of people who said that they couldn't, shouldn't or wouldn't take their idea forward and turn it into reality.

How many people turn round at that point and give up? Too many. However, you aren't one of those people any more. You have courage and inner strength that you are going to turn up to help you find what it is that *you* want and to help you keep on track as you set out on the journey to get it.

EXERCISE

Negative voice

I want you to tune into that negative inner voice that you hear from time to time – you know, the one that stops you from having more happiness, fun or success. If more than one such message pops into your head then that is fine: Write down whatever comes to mind from your negative inner voice right now.

Now I want you to really look at the structure of what you have written. I'm expecting there to be lots of negative phrasing. The next part of the exercise is to rewrite the statements with a positive intention. So if you had written, "I can't afford it," then a positive way of writing it would be, "How can I afford it?"

You may need to play with the words and the formation until you are completely happy but you are looking for a statement that gives you power, motivation and excitement about the possibilities that await you. You don't need to know how you will get to where you want to be; you need to be willing to be open to the fact that you can get there.

I hope by now you have some understanding of how you've become the person that you are today. I am choosing to believe that the stories and experiences I have shared with you have given you food for thought and have reassured you that the things you have been thinking and feeling about yourself and about life are completely normal and that millions of people on the planet share your view too.

SUMMARY

No one sets out to sabotage themselves or their opportunities yet the tough reality is that no matter what life or anyone throws at us, it is how we react and respond that defines the life we then go on to lead. In getting real clarity on who you are as an individual and how you came to be at this point is massive progress in being able to decide what you might like to do next. Because you have given up regretting or blaming yourself for past decisions and have become comfortable that it was simply research means that you focus your efforts and energy on the future, which is still up for grabs, rather than wasting it on stuff that has already occurred and is unchangeable. Use your positive statements to start coming up with a plan on what you are going to do next and be excited for what the future holds.

Chapter 10

TAKING ACTION

WITH

DOUBLE ESPRESSO WITH A CHOCOLATE CHIP MUFFIN

So what is going to stop you from taking action?

- Fear of failure?

- Fear of rejection?

- A belief you are not worth it?

The simple truth that I know and I definitely see when I work with my clients is that people want to feel 'good' – it is that simple.

Some of my greatest success as a coach is getting my clients to remember what 'good' feels like and then getting them to practise finding that feeling inside themselves so they know where it is and can access it when they need it.

My biggest challenge was a client who believed that they had never felt good. Well I guarantee that just like them you have an imagination, so if you are thinking, "Yes, I also have not got a memory that I can associate with the concept of feeling 'good'", then the question you need to ask yourself is simple: "What would I want good to feel like?"

EXERCISE

Feeling good

Write a list of all the things you would expect to get from feeling good. Include feeling sensations, and aspects of body language that people would notice about you.

When my client Lara did this exercise she said:

> For me I want to have more fun in my life, so the feeling I want is a lightness in my thinking. I want to be laughing and smiling more. And I want a sense of feeling playful – not being too grown up. Childlike rather than childish.

I want to be able to enjoy myself without feeling like I'm always doing virtual risk assessments for every situation I am in. I want to be able to enjoy life at face value and see the really simple pleasures that are there in front of me that I normally miss because of concentrating too much on being a grown up.

By creating a clear message to herself, she suddenly started to notice opportunities to have more fun. Previously, she would decline invites to activities that she had never tried before simply because she believed she wouldn't be any good at the activity or she felt afraid. What she noticed was that her friends stopped asking her to everything because they believed she would say 'no' and a sense of rejection began to creep in when she heard they had been off doing stuff when she had not been invited. Yet when she told her friends that she had made a commitment to herself to have more fun and to try new things they started to invite her to all the activities they were off doing and the more she said 'yes' the more fun she began to have. Of course, there were activities and experiences she enjoyed more than others, but by holding on to the research mantra it didn't matter.

These experiences don't have to cost anything as many of my clients have found. Many executives work very long hours and find getting the balance with family difficult, but finishing work early to pick up the children from school or arranging an impromptu picnic on a sunny day charge the batteries very effectively.

EXERCISE

Wheel of life

Here is the wheel of life again. However, knowing what you now know having read the rest of the book I want you to set yourself a couple of goals on changing the two aspects that you feel will have the biggest effect in making you move forward from wherever you are stuck.

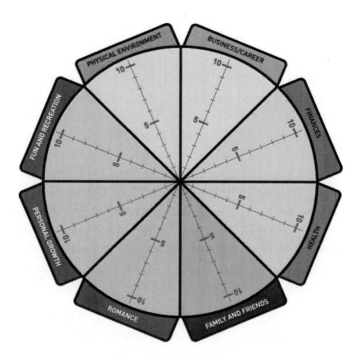

The two areas of my life I want to work on are:

1)

2)

When I think about

(write whatever was the first area), I recognise the belief I have had that has been holding me back is

However, I now realise a better belief to have is:

In the spirit of positive intention I commit to do the following two things immediately:

1.

2.

....

....

....

I am excited about the possibilities this change will have because:

....

....

....

....

The people who can help me achieve this are (make sure you include yourself):

....

....

....

....

I commit to start working on this

....

When I think about

....

(write whatever was the second area), I recognise the belief I have had that has been holding me back is:

....

....

However, I now realise a better belief to have is:

In the spirit of positive intention I commit to do the following two things immediately:

1.

2.

I am excited about the possibilities this change will have because:

The people who can help me achieve this are (make sure you include yourself):

....

....

....

....

I commit to start working on this:

....

Now I am clear that I control what the future holds I am excited and motivated to make the change.

Signed:

....

One of the things that I encourage you to do is to share your commitments with someone you trust who will help support you and help you stay on track. This is the role that I play for my clients; when I meet up with them or talk to them on the phone, I will check how they are doing against their goals, where they have taken action and if they haven't what has stopped them.

It is natural to believe that making a change will be difficult, especially if you have had years of running the same patterns and you have got used to being where you are. However, if you have decided that there are things that you would like to work on then break them down into little steps so they manageable.

Some clients find they need to create mini-goals within their bigger goals so that they feel in control as they see and notice the change begin to occur. The other thing we will do in coaching is review what is and isn't working and discuss the idea that it is simply the art of research and having the ability to tweak and change your plan or your goals as things start moving forward for you.

In the coaching session we will talk about things that may be a barrier, after all my clients can be honest about what has stopped them taking this action before because they know themselves better than anyone. We then create possible solutions to get over the barriers or blockers so that if they do occur my clients know what they can do to keep moving forward.

EXERCISE

· Barriers

What are the possible barriers or blockers to you being able to make progress on the two areas you have decided to work on?

....

....

....

....

How can I get around these blockers creatively to keep moving forward?

....

....

....

....

Who can help you if you get really stuck?

....

....

....

....

If you struggle to come up with solutions to the blockers think about what the opposite behaviour may be – sometimes doing something completely different may be the game changer for us. So if your normal behaviour is to play it safe then think about what taking a risk would look like.

SUMMARY

Feeling that you are stuck and believing you cannot do anything about it is something that the majority of the western population experiences at some point in their lives. Out of that group more than half do nothing proactively to improve or change their circumstances; they sit and wait for life to send them opportunities and then, because they are not necessarily tuned in to them, unsurprisingly they are missed. They tend to have a glass half empty mindset so instead of looking for positives or success they look for negatives and failure. It should be no surprise to hear that people tend to see what they are looking for.

All of my clients fit into the other half of the population because they do proactively take action to change whatever it is they are unhappy with or about. The speed with which they achieve their goals varies but they all have achieved the changes that they wanted by being clear on which areas of their life could be improved and by establishing what they wanted that change to look like – even if they had no idea how they would achieve it.

For example, I remember wanting to do more work on a global basis but I didn't define what that work would look like and where overseas it would be. Yet within two months of that thought

I had met a new contact who offered me the opportunity to work as an associate with them training leaders and executives from blue chip organisations. And just six months after having my thought I was standing in a five-star hotel in Malaysia delivering training to a group of senior leaders of a Fortune 500 company. Yet I truly believe that if I had not been specifically looking out for the opportunities to achieve my goals then I would not have spotted what was being offered or have had the courage to take that next step.

Chapter 11

ONWARDS AND UPWARDS

WITH

CHAMPAGNE AND CHOCOLATE TRUFFLES

Congratulations on everything you have achieved in your life so far. I hope in working through the exercises in this book and reading my client stories you now know yourself better and along the way realised that whatever you have experienced makes you the amazing person you are today. Everything that has happened in the past is research to help you create the plan you need for the goals and success that awaits you in the future. You by now will be clear what bits of research have worked for you and empowered you and what doesn't work and that you can therefore let go of and move on from.

If you have realised that you have been wearing a mask and if you have felt that you are a fraud and have experienced pangs of guilt in the past then from now on you are no different to many masked superheroes that have gone before you – Zorro, Superman, Spiderman and Wonder Woman, to name a few. Remember that all of these characters had alter-egos – and you are no different.

You have everything you need in this book to help you decide your immediate goals, what is going to make you happy, where you get your beliefs from and where in your life you would like more happiness. I told you I would cram a lot in when we first met at the start.

If you are feeling anxious, or doubting your ability to do this on your own, then just keep going back to sections in the book that gave you the most insight, redo the exercises, especially the wheel of life exercise and the happiness quiz, as you take steps forward. Think about the people who can help you, too. My clients have me and friends, family members and colleagues but it requires them to be honest. Remember the insight that my client Tom (see chapter 4) had when he feared that people would reject him and ridicule him for not presenting himself in the most authentic way. If you don't share stuff with the people who are closest to you then don't be surprised that they don't notice when you need their help – especially if the message they are receiving is, "It is all fine."

If you are feeling scared and a little bit doubtful that you will be able to make the changes you need then I want to reassure you that change is something feared by at least half the population. In addition, if you plan and control what the change will be and are very clear about what your positive intention is behind the change then it should be a lot less scary, particularly as you can move along at your pace.

Be conscious of the thoughts/feelings/behaviour triangle. The more positive and empowered you are feeling and are acting then the better quality thoughts you will have. So if you are feeling particularly disempowered and of low energy then don't put yourself under pressure to make big decisions. Wait until your thinking changes (as it always will) and then take the actions that feel right.

Remember that the point of doing any of this work is to be happier, more fulfilled and to be no longer stuck. So if you start doing something and it doesn't fulfil one of the three goals – stop and try something different.

Some of my clients tell me that they aren't creative at coming up with activities that they believe would enable them to have more fun or happiness, so here are a few suggestions that over the years have been shown to bring great results. I hope there will be something here that gets you moving forward to have the happiness in life that you deserve.

Activities for fun or happiness

Let the music play

If I need energy then I will reach for my iPod and get some pop or rock on, anything with a good beat that will lift my mood or allow me to have a good sing-along. If I need to relax then I will opt for something classical or gentle that will soothe me and allow me to chill out.

Find a film

There are so many great films that can make you feel good depending on what you want at the time. Some of my favourites because of their messages include: *It's a Wonderful Life* (1946, directed by Frank Capra), *In Pursuit of Happyness* (2006, directed by Gabriele Muccino), *Runaway Bride* (1999, directed by Garry Marshall), *The Lord of the Rings* (2001-3, directed by Peter Jackson), *Hitch* (2005, directed by Andy Tennant), *Good Will Hunting* (1997, directed by Gus Van Sant), *Dead Poets Society* (1989, directed by Andy Weir) and *Sliding Doors* (1998, directed by Peter Howitt).

It's amazing the resilience that we have within us, if only we allow ourselves the chance to be the best version of ourselves. See if you can create of a list of feel-good films that you enjoy. Pop one on and watch it whenever you need a lift.

Smell the flowers

I mean this literally. There are some wonderful scents that can lift your mood. My particular favourites are freesias and jasmine – it makes me smile when I catch their scents. Which smells make you smile? I remember as a little girl that my mum always wore a particular perfume when I first went to school and as I felt so horribly homesick at school she would spray a bit of that perfume on a tissue that I would tuck into my little purse and could get out and smell if I felt frightened or needed reassurance. I would always feel much better immediately.

Run a bath

I know that most of us are conscious of doing what we can to protect the environment and so take showers these days, but there is something really indulgent in running a bath and lighting some candles to go around the side. That dim, flickering light is almost hypnotic. I have a few clients who at different times have been struggling with big decisions and this simple activity has allowed them the right mental space to think through their options and come up with an answer that they were happy with. I know whenever I've done it myself it has usually meant I've had a fabulous night's sleep.

Bake something

There is something wonderfully therapeutic about creating something yourself. I love the smell of baking in the oven – bread, cakes or savoury dishes. The other benefit of baking is that it allows you to invite or include others in helping you to enjoy the outcome of your endeavours.

One of the funniest occasions of attempting to bake was when I tried to make a chocolate cake and sadly misread the recipe. I used plain flour in the mixture with no raising agent. My friends howled when my 'biscuit' came out of the oven. The thought of that experience still makes me smile now.

Arrange a night out

It can be easy to let your life be consumed with work or by being a parent and to forget that you are a person in your own right. Being lonely isn't good, and if you are ever ill or sad it won't be work that will comfort you – it will be your friends or family. So even if it has been a while, invite some of your friends to meet you for a drink and if that goes well you have the option to extend the get-together to dinner.

Be grateful

What are the things that you are most grateful you have in your life? Perhaps it is material stuff – a car? a house? a job? Perhaps it is being healthy? Having friends? Having family? In a way it does not matter what it is that you are grateful for so long as you recognise that gratitude. Sometimes we can be too busy worrying about what we don't have to notice all of the things that we do have.

I am alive

This one I borrow from my friend Richard Wilkins. When he talks to big groups he always uses this story.

I want you to imagine that you have just found out that you have won £5,000,000 on the lottery. How would you behave? What would you be saying? I'd hope that you would be whooping and hollering with joy. Now imagine that the choice you have to make is to win £5,000,000 on the lottery or not be dead. Which option would you choose? I expect you would say, "To not be dead." After all, if you were dead then you couldn't enjoy the money anyway. So, that must mean that not being dead is worth more than £5,000,000? Yet most of us wake up every morning and don't even notice that we are alive. Celebrate waking up.

Dream jar

I spotted this idea a few years ago and loved it. All you need is some stationery, an empty glass jar and possibly something to cover the jar with if you want to exercise your creative muscles. I covered mine with some pretty stickers. Every day in a period that you should set for yourself (it may be a whole calendar year from 1 January to 31 December or perhaps just a month) take a minute at the end of the day to think about one nice thing that happened to you during that day and write it down on a piece of paper, fold it up and put it in your jar. Tip out the contents at the end the period and read the pieces of paper. It is amazing how good those memories make you feel. On days when I struggle to think of something I may write down a quotation, saying or lyric that I like.

Nothing for best

When I was little my mum would buy me clothes that were deemed to be 'my best' and I was only allowed to wear them on special occasions, which was sad really as they never got used very much. I'll confess that even as a grown-up I carried this practice on until I read an article supposedly about an old man who was packing up the belongings of his recently departed wife, including silk underwear that was 'for best' and had never been worn and perfume that he loved but she had only worn on special occasions, and counselled that it was best to not have anything for best: Use it every day and enjoy all of your possessions. From that moment on I followed those wise words and I have shared the message with numerous clients over the years, too. I remember working with a lovely female manager who had a fabulously expensive handbag that she used only on her birthday and at Christmas. She was frightened of damaging it or wearing out the leather. Yet she recognised the enjoyment that she got on those rare days that she used it. When I asked her how it would be if she could have that feeling every day she said that of course she would like that. The solution was simple. We laughed about it after she decided that she would use her gorgeous bag every day and enjoy it. I bumped into her five years after that and she was still using that bag and it still looked as good as it had when she had first bought it. You see quality-made things do last and the smile and enjoyment she had had over that period was priceless. So don't wait to use any of your stuff that you think is special – you never know when you may not be here to enjoy them.

Have a rainy day pot

I remember when the £2 coin first came out and it was a novelty to have one in my purse, so I used to save them in a pot and then when it was full I'd count them out and treat myself to something nice. I have taught my daughters to save 20ps or 50ps in the hope that it will teach them the value of saving and having the enjoyment of being able to treat themselves to something nice. It can be a really lovely surprise to find out how much some pots and money boxes can hold. It can also give you a real sense of achievement when you realise that you have fulfilled a task.

Get outdoors

How often do you notice all of the amazing sights that are right outside your door? It may be that you are so busy or distracted you just can't see what is there. Now while I hope that you aren't feeling depressed or subdued, it is a well-known fact that when people do feel like that they often look down and try to use their body language to make themselves small. When you are in this frame of mind the quality of the decisions you make are usually quite poor and on occasions you may come to regret things. One simple thing you can do is to change your physiology. Put your shoulders back and look up. I have used this technique with many clients who are feeling depressed or who are finding things difficult. When we put our shoulders back and look up we feel completely different, our breathing changes from being short, and occasionally quite shallow, breaths to being full, big breaths so we are getting more oxygen in our system. You can obviously do this inside and it will be effective, but I always notice that my mood and that of my clients improves so much more if you walk around outside. Perhaps it's the mix of fresh air and the change of environment that allows you to have such an improved perspective but I know the decisions you make when you feel positive are of a much better quality than when you are feeling down and small.

Add some colour

Now being a trained image consultant I'm naturally going to suggest that you should have a colour analysis with a trained consultant. I remember when I first learned the technique that I was astounded at how different I could feel when I wore different colours and looked at myself in the mirror. The benefit of properly knowing which colours suit you will save you time and money and will guarantee that you feel fantastic. Between the ages of 25 and 50 men and women spend on average £60-£80,000 on their clothes yet they may only wear half of their wardrobe because they inadvertently buy things that don't suit them and when they wear them they don't feel good. Wearing the right colours positively affects how we feel and how we are seen. I'd also encourage you to get a bodyline analysis so you know exactly the right cut and styles that will work in the best way for your body scale and shape. It doesn't matter where you buy your clothes from; I had a very savvy client who went shopping in charity shops in very affluent areas and once she got to know the makes that worked best for her body shape she started using eBay and was able to buy designer clothes for a fraction of the price and she looked and felt amazing.

Have a vision

One of the tools I love using with individual clients and teams is a vision board. As you will have seen through the use of some of the stories in the book, in order to move on when you feel stuck, you need a plan or a goal to be aiming for. A vision board is a fun way of getting some wishes and inspiration of what your goals and intentions are for yourself.

Get a load of magazines together and then flick through them, ripping out any pictures or headlines that you like. Stick them randomly on a large piece of paper and notice any messages that you are telling yourself.

I did this many years ago when I was still employed as an HR professional. The pictures I put on my vision board included a picture of an Oscar, pictures of a tropical island, a nice car, a larger house, someone running their own company and lots of times with friends and family. Over a period of 18 months from completing that vision board I was recognised as the UK's Executive Coach of the Year by one of the coaching professional bodies and I had to attend a glamorous awards ceremony in London to collect my award. I got the chance to take my girls to China, Lapland and then Borneo in the space of nine months. I had some building work done on my house to make better use of the space. I changed my car to a newer model that very few people had. All of these things may have happened regardless of doing my vision board – but I choose to believe that because I created a vision of what I wanted I then noticed the opportunities that were there to help me get what I wanted.

Get some balance

A lot of my clients are in very senior positions in their companies and a topic that comes up quite regularly during the course of our sessions is the pressure to spend more and more time working and where they do have families the guilt that they feel about spending time away from them. Have you ever heard anyone who is terminally ill saying, "I really wish I could spend more time at work"? Spend more time with the people that you know bring out the best in you.

Try out new stuff

You are never too old to learn something new. Remember Becca (see chapter 3) who wanted to do 40 new things in a year? Yes, she had a nervous breakdown, she got divorced and she had to have her cat put down, which were all very difficult experiences, but there were the 35-36 happy and enjoyable things that she did do. If she had not set herself the goal she may not have done anything. She inspired me to be more adventurous and now I aim for something more modest and try to do 4-12 new things a year, which can mean just one new thing every three months. They do not have to be hard – read a new book, go somewhere new for dinner or meet some new people.

Ask for help

Like my clients you will have things that you are really good at and that you enjoy doing and you will have things that you don't believe you are skilled at and that you will try and put off for as long as possible.

Learn to ask for help with the things you know you are not so good at. A couple of my clients have bartered their skills for my skills and it has worked incredibly well. I have had the benefit of a cleaner, gardener and decorator all as a trade for coaching time.

It's OK to not be OK

Some people are naturally more sensitive than others. This is not a sign of weakness; it is a reflection of the person you are. There are times when all of us go to the dark part of our persona where we mentally beat ourselves up, or when we have very low energy. If you are there or you recognise this place then that is completely fine. However, just know that when you are there it is only your thoughts that are taking you there and they will pass.

Spin your negative thinking

When you have a negative thought or belief, ask yourself, "What if the real case is actually the opposite of that thought?" Spend some time imagining the flip side and see if you can find any evidence to support that.

Acting as if

Sometimes we hold ourselves back because we believe we are missing a skill or attribute. We let the negative voice in our heads feed our beliefs. One of the things I love doing with my clients is getting them to identify which attribute or skill they believe they are missing and then once they are clear on that I then get them to think about someone they know who shows up using the trait they believe they are missing. We talk about what they notice to be different about how that person behaves and what things they imagine that person may be saying to themselves. When they are really clear on all of those aspects I get them to behave *as if* they are the role model they have been thinking about. Generally, the more practice they get acting *as if* the more they feel as if they have that skill or attribute.

If you are feeling stuck then do something different

Many clients will speak about how in certain situations they feel stuck and they feel like they don't know what to do. Quite often they have been trying the same things as a means to move forward but (unsurprisingly) have not been getting different results.

If you do what you have always done then you will get what you have always got. My encouragement in this situation is for them to decide what the opposite behaviour would be from what they have been trying. Quite often trying something new or different is sufficient to move the situation forward one way or another.

Write a bucket list

What are all the things you would like to do before you kick the bucket? Be as wild and creative as you like. There is a great film called *The Bucket List* (2007, directed by Rob Reiner) with Morgan Freeman and Jack Nicholson which is about two men who know they are dying and who set out to have as much fun as they can in the time they have left.

Write a list of everything you have achieved in the last six months

We often do not give ourselves enough credit for all that we do. So just focus on the last six months and write down everything you have achieved. If this feels a challenge because you have been having a tough time, give yourself credit for carrying on and being there for all the people who rely on you. Think about everything you have learned about yourself because of those experiences.

Write a letter bragging about your success

You will need pen and paper and a timer before you start. Set the timer for 20 minutes. Prepare yourself to write non-stop until the timer goes off.

I want you to imagine that it is about six months from now and you have settled down to write a letter to a friend. Your letter should have the aim of bringing them up to date with all the exciting and successful things you have been up to.

Write without really thinking. It doesn't matter how ridiculous or implausible your thoughts are – just go for it. Start your letter with: *I have had the most amazing six months of my life. I am so happy and excited and wanted to bring you up to date with all that has been going on for me.*

Put the letter away when you have finished it and in six

months' time get it out and read it back to yourself and see if any of your letter has come true.

SUMMARY

Many of my clients start by telling me that they never expected to be in a situation where they felt that they needed the help of a coach. I share with them that I never intended to be a single mum who ran her own business yet this is where I am and I don't regret any of the experiences I have had because I know that they have made me the person that I am today. Because of my personal development I know the benefits of being able to sort the good research from the bad experiences; the former becomes a resource into which I can dip whenever I need it and with experiences I don't enjoy then I make a mental note to not repeat them.

Be proud of who you are and what you have achieved and take heart that you will find your way of moving from being stuck to being inspired, energised and EMPOWERED!

ABOUT THE AUTHOR

Anne Mulliner is an award-winning executive coach and leadership development expert who works with clients all over the world, sharing her passion for getting them to access their full potential and live life at 10 out of 10. She is an accredited master coach, behaviour specialist and image consultant. She lives in the UK with her two daughters.

email: anne@jdicreativesolutions.co.uk
web: www.jdicreativesolutions.co.uk